S0-AHA-973

N O W
WHAT

JR HARDING
WITH ERIKA RICHARDS-HARDING

SokheChapke Publishing, Inc.

Published by:

SokheChapke Publishing, Inc., ©

P.O Box 21161

Tallahassee, FL 32316

545 East Tennessee St., Suite 200-A

Tallahassee, FL 32308

Telephone: 866-711-5984

Email: info@sokhechapkepublishing.com

Website: sokhechapkepublishing.com

Copyright ©: 2011 Dr. JR Harding and Erika Richards-Harding

Now What by Dr. JR Harding with Erika Richards-Harding

All rights reserved. No part of this publication may be reproduced, stored in a retrieval system, or transmitted in any form or by any means, electronic, mechanical, photocopy, recording, or otherwise, without the prior written permission of Dr. JR Harding and Erika Richards-Harding. SokheChapke books and other publications are available through most bookstores.

To contact SokheChapke Publishing, please write to us at 545 E. Tennessee Street, Suite 200-A, Tallahassee, FL 32308 or call 850-688-9694 or 866-711-5984 (toll free).

Discounts on volume purchases of SokheChapke books are available. For more information, call 850-688-9694 or 866-711-5984 and ask for customer services.

ISBN 978-1463604363

Published and printed in the United States of America

Table of Contents

Acknowledgements

This work has been a long time coming. I had flirted with the idea, talked with friends and family, for over 20 years, and finally put pen to paper! I would like to formally and profoundly express my deep appreciation to my lovely wife Erika Richards-Harding. Without her assistance, without her encouragement, and without her pushing this work, it would never have been accomplished.

I am deeply indebted to my family by blood and marriage. Their unbridled love, sacrifices, and commitment to my independent journey is simply priceless. Without their continued support, courage for "tough love," and ability to envision a future beyond the here and now, I would be unable to share my story with all of you.

It is simply impossible for Erika and me to specifically and publicly thank everyone who has contributed hundreds of hours of encouragement and assistance during this journey. There have literally been hundreds of individuals that include my friends, personal care assistants, administrative assistants, coaches, administrators and strangers, who have helped shape who I am today, each deserving of individual accolades. This work has been a team effort. Please know that I will always be indebted to you for your friendship, willingness to overcome barriers, and your graciousness in providing a second chance even in times when I was undeserving.

Living with a significant disability, as the Americans with Disabilities Act so properly expresses, "is natural" and no physical and/or attitudinal barrier cannot be overcome because of who we are as Americans. Each of us understands, intuitively, that no matter what, each of us has the right and responsibility to pursue "life, liberty and the pursuit of happiness."

Finally, Erika and I express appreciation to those who helped us cross the finish line. I must thank Ms. Randi Gingerich, at the University of West Florida and SokheChapke Publishing.

Introduction

'll never know why it happened. I will never understand what forces were behind it. I do know that it happened instantly and would have a lifelong effect. Perhaps I didn't take life seriously. Perhaps I was irresponsible, or maybe I was just simply not respectful of my gifts. What I do know is that the vicissitude began...

In hindsight, this voyage into the unknown would become a blessing in disguise. In time and through personal challenges, I would find my calling in life. My passion for independence, self-sufficiency and self-reliance was developed from constantly asking "Now what?" and continuously setting little goals that could and would be achieved.

This is my story, a true story as I recall it. Some of the names have been changed to protect the innocent and the not so innocent. So now what are you waiting for?

JR

Prologue

There is no prescription given to you by the doctor when leaving the hospital with a newborn baby. I believe that most parents strive for the best. I had the privilege or the curse of raising two boys. Each day was a surprise. You bathe them, feed them, dress them, send them out the door, and pray that they return home to you safely.

In the case of JR, I was accustomed to emergency rooms, doctors, and nurses. Our first incident came at the age of four with a metal shard adhered to his cornea. At age five, he showed up with a pussy willow lodged in his ear canal. At six, he hit a brick wall head-on with his bicycle. I only recognized him because of the clothes he was wearing that morning. At seven, a baseball bat collided with the side of his mouth, and the first fourteen stitches were sewn inside. At nine, there was a dislocated elbow from jumping out of a swing. By age ten, we had an understanding that he was to get cleaned up, stitched up or whatever necessary before returning home.

The fall of 1983 had begun well for us, compared to previous years. My husband was promoted to full colonel, and we were stationed at Fort Campbell in Kentucky. JR was beginning his senior year at Culver Military Academy. Not only was he going to graduate (just), but there was also talk of athletic scholarships for college. JR's brother was starting his sophomore year at The Hill School. I fondly recall boastfully sharing with one of my friends at the Officers' Club that life was good. I had earned my battle stripes, like my husband, raising the boys. But the rumbling in the clouds above did not prepare me for the lightning bolt about to tear apart my perfect mortal world. On the morning of September 26th, returning home from church, I ran into the house to answer the phone. A cold chill ran up my spine, and I turned to my husband overwhelmed with fear, "We have to go to Chicago..."

1

Life was easy. I was popular, possessed multiple varsity letters, and was good looking. Like a lot of sixteen year-olds, I was self-centered and a bit of a trouble maker, but all in all I had a kind heart, was loyal to my friends, and was a well-meaning kid. The tragedy was like a scene out of one of the Greek mythologies where the gods would toy with mortals' lives for entertainment. Without warning one of the gods swooped down into my life and said, "Try this."

Friday night, September 24, 1983, was the night of the sixth game of the season for the Culver Eagles football team. We were 5-0 and playing the regional powerhouse, Heritage Christian, for the right to advance to the district state finals. Our team had made its mark by running the option left and running the option right; both backs had already broken 1,000 yards. I stood just less than six feet five inches, weighed 220 pounds, and was the starting left offensive tackle for the second year in a row. The entire line stood over six feet and weighed anywhere from 200 to 235 pounds. We were fast, strong, and agile! Our strength came from getting off the ball quicker and running through our opponents. We were playing our hearts out against Heritage. It was the fourth quarter with one minute to go, third and six, and we were down by three. We had two downs and 40 yards to go to win the game. The coach called an unpredictable play action pass to the tight end. The call surprised our team, we could run like the wind, but passing was not our strength. However, being obedient military cadets, we did as we were told despite not liking the call. On three, the ball was hiked. The fake to the fullback went seamlessly, the tight end came across the middle, the ball was thrown high and floated into the hands of the awaiting safety – an interception! Since they now had the ball, I could use my hands. So, I threw the outside linebacker to the side and went for the kill. The safety's attempt to beat me to the outside corner failed. We connected, went airborne, and flew across the far sidelines. Just as I was getting off of him, his teammates surrounded us. I didn't retreat. Instead I made a competitive snarl, "Not on my watch!"

He looked right at me, smirked, and said, "You don't have the ball anymore." He was right; we were on defense with only 30 seconds left in the game. His team protected the ball and just like that, the game was over.

We would return to our locker room with our heads down and to a dismal silence. We had done everything coach had asked; we had played our best, but victory was not to be ours and we felt the agony of defeat. Even worse, each of us began to comprehend that there would be no state playoffs for us, just a winning season.

As we boarded the bus to return to campus, coach authoritatively told us that the team meeting and post-game briefing would be at 8:00 a.m. the following morning. I didn't listen to him, nor did I care about any meeting. After all, I was still grieving from the loss. I spent most of the ride home crying with one of my best friends, Mike. We wanted nothing more than to go to the playoffs, especially since the Eagles had not been there in several seasons.

Mike was a fellow senior, a fellow varsity letterman, and one of my best friends. He understood, at a personal level, how painful losing an important game was, despite playing one's heart out. We did what buddies do. We talked; we picked the game apart play by play. We concluded it wasn't our fault, nor was it our night.

When 8:00 a.m. rolled around, I did wake up. My eyes were swollen and my ego crushed. The last thing I needed to do was to hear coach point out that we missed that hit or didn't make that block. Instead, I wanted to redirect my energies, find something fresh to turn my mood around. At 16, there was no better way to do that than to go on a date. I called my girlfriend Lori and made plans for the evening. She was excited and happy

2

because during football season, there wasn't much time for a social life.

The night began with dinner at the local burger shack on the corner of campus overlooking the lake. From there we went to the auditorium for a Saturday night movie. We didn't mingle with a lot of our friends, but rather selfishly enjoyed one another. Lori and I sat in the back corner of the theater, dimly lit, holding hands and flirting without displaying too much PDA. I scored a lot of points by taking her to one of the hottest new releases, *Flash Dance.* After the movie came to an end, it was a little after 10:00 p.m. and I walked Lori back to her dormitory.

Boarding school had strict rules, and everyone had to be accounted for by 11:00 p.m. Because it was already 10:30 p.m., I kissed her good night and I began my walk back to the other side of campus. It was a peaceful walk. I kept daydreaming about the wonderful evening, thinking about when I was going to get lucky in the near future. The football game and the loss were far from my mind. I was in a world all to myself, a dream state. Perhaps this explains why I did not see Jake, the middle linebacker, come out of the shadows. Right behind him was Hawk, the other offensive tackle. They were co-captains of the football team and had been anointed positional power and prestige by the coaches. They had not been elected by the team. In truth, Jake and I had never been friends; we only tolerated each other on the field. He was extremely pissed that I had blown off the team meeting earlier that morning. Immediately, he was in my face, pushing and shoving me, screaming, "How could you embarrass me? What kind of example are you sending to the underclassmen?" and punched me in the mouth.

My head switched gears. I didn't need this kind of bullshit — not this early in my senior year. It was stupid; it was adolescent nonsense. Jake and Hawk, however, wanted to teach me a lesson. Despite my throbbing jaw, I had the courage to turn the other cheek and started to walk away. Maybe I was afraid. Maybe instinctively, I knew there was no value in this dispute. For whatever reason, that's the decision I made.

Nonetheless, before I even took my second step, Hawk grabbed me from behind, lifted me into the air, and body-slammed me into the hard Indiana dirt. I landed awkwardly, and was unable to break my fall because I had no idea it was coming; Hawk took me by surprise. The impact of my body against the ground was devastating. My full body weight plus the force of the throw on the unforgiving ground crushed my spinal cord. My reflexes wouldn't work! I couldn't move! Jake kicked me.

"Get up you sissy," he said aggressively.

"I can't," I told him with pain in my voice.

They didn't believe me. Hawk and Jake tried to stand me up. My legs went out from under me, and they realized in a fraction of a second that something had gone seriously wrong.

"My God, he's right!" Jake exclaimed as he pushed my body forward then watched me fall back like a sack of potatoes.

They were in shock, and all they could do was stand with their arms in the air looking clueless. I knew that I had to take charge of the situation.

"Get some help," I cried. "Good God, get somebody now!"

They bolted to call the doctor and EMT's. At the same time, a crowd began to assemble around me. I was staring blindly into the night sky, expressionless and helpless. Out of the many faces staring down on me, I recognized Ralph, one of my good friends. I told him that I couldn't move my legs. I was trying to stay cool. I knew I was hurt; I just didn't know how bad. I was doing my best to stay conscious and not have the shock overcome me. Ralph assured me that help was on its way.

Suddenly, my world was being thrown into a blender. The doctor from the infirmary arrived; the ambulance from town started to unload a stretcher; people were shouting and running in hysterics. Voices from the crowd roared out, "Is he drunk? Did he overdose? My God, what happened here?" Everyone turned to Jake and Hawk. They said nothing. I don't know if I passed out or just couldn't recall the following events

4

exactly because I've blocked them out somehow, but in spite of being tied down to a stretcher. I could hear blades swirling in the air above me. People were scurrying   everywhere. They soon became ants on an ant hill busy at work below me. I was being lifted up in a helicopter. I could hear the loud thumping of the blades beating through the air.

The only thing I felt was a pressure on my shoulder. I don't know how he convinced the commandant to let him come with me, but Ralph did the impossible, and comforted me.

"Ralph," I said, "Don't leave me!"

Slowly, I saw the stars in the sky fade away. The painkiller or shock or both took me into complete darkness. I arrived at the trauma center at Chicago Memorial. They tell me it was a 30-minute flight.

2

I later awoke in a hospital bed. I could feel the restraints around my neck. All I could see were the blaring fluorescent lights above me and the drab off-white ceiling.

"Hello? Hello?" I gasped. All I could hear was the pitter patter of shoes across the floor.

"Doctor, come quickly, he's awake," a nurse shouted. She quickly attended to my vitals.

Why is it that when you're darn good and awake, doctors find it necessary to pierce your pupils with a blinding light and stretch your eyeballs?

"My eyes are fine," I told him.

"That they are," the nurse smiled. "You have magical blue eyes."

I felt warm knowing that I could still get a reaction from the ladies.

Immediately the cognitive tests began from the doctor.

"Do you know where you are?"

"Yes, the hospital."

"Do you know what happened?"

"I'm paralyzed."

"How old are you?"

"Sixteen."

"Ah, but tomorrow you're turning seventeen."

Three days had passed since the incident.

After I passed the initial cognitive test, the nurse began the sensory exam. The nurse pricked my cheek with a pin and asked if I could feel it. She began pricking down the entire length of my body, testing my reflexes. As the pin began to go south of my chest, I found myself uncertain...did I feel the pin, or did I just think I felt it?

Sadly, they were phantom feelings. I lay in bed struggling to move, thinking that my fingers had twitched, or that one leg had crossed over the next. I was certain it had happened, but could never have these actions validated. It would take hundreds of pin pricks for me to differentiate what was and wasn't real. These brief interactions with the physician and nurse consumed what little strength I had. I succumbed to the power of the morphine, and the drab off-white ceiling faded from sight as my eyes slid shut.

The next time I awoke, I found my father standing at the foot of my ICU bed. He had traveled all the way from Kentucky where he was serving as a brigade commander for the 101st Airborne Division. He stared at me with an unexplainable look. His face wore pain, frustration, anger, yet also love. As a career army officer with four years of combat experience, he had been conditioned to deal with blood, body parts, and death. Nothing, however, prepared him to handle the tragedy before him involving his eldest son who carried his name.

Besides the look of uncertainty, I will never forget his question: "Now what?"

At that moment, I felt as if I had let him down. So, not wanting to disappoint him further, I optimistically answered, "I want to graduate – graduate with my class." With this response, a mission began for my father and me. We had a goal, a purpose, and a focus to guide us into an unknown future.

The routine of life and personal responsibilities do not stop just because a tragedy occurs. Since my parents had to work, they returned to Fort Campbell, and I remained in the ICU at Northwestern Memorial Hospital. In their stead, my grandmother moved from West Palm Beach, Florida, to Chicago. She would monitor my progress. She would occupy the side of my bed for what limited time the ICU would permit visitors until my mother could return on the weekends. She would keep the family informed and remind me daily that I was loved!

The physician explained that I had crushed the fifth cervical vertebra (approximately where the neck and shoulders meet).

"In order to fuse the vertebras back together, we had to carve four inches off your shin bone and use it like a medical welding mechanism," he explained. "The use of your own bone as a graphing tool should help prevent rejection and more likely guarantee successful healing of your spinal cord. It's kind of like a splint for your back bones."

I was grateful for the doctor's input. I knew I was paralyzed when the injury happened, but I hadn't understood the extent of it. To me, paralysis meant that I could not move. I failed to appreciate that there are differences between paraplegics, quadriplegics, and the variations in-betweens. The doctor explained to me that the level of paralysis for the patient/me, is directly related to the injury level around the spinal cord and the amount of post injury damage to the neurological system. Because my injury occurred at the fifth cervical level of the spinal cord, the result was quadriplegia affecting all four of my limbs. It was made clear to me that my spinal cord would heal, but I would lose some mobility to both the left and right angles of my neck's rotation. It would take time for me to understand fully what a C-5 injury meant because the permanency of the neurological damage was uncertain. I chose to pass each day as if my condition was temporary. After all, this approach made sense to me; every other time I damaged my body, I had recovered.

The doctor also informed me that I would have to wear a cumbersome metal neck brace for the next six months and in time, I would adapt to a new way of life. Because I was a former varsity athlete, he didn't foresee any complications and expected a three-week transition into the rehab stage of recovery. We could begin as soon as I was stable.

I was in a good mood, ready to face rehab, and really convinced that my condition was temporary. But the next morning, strapped to the striker frame bed being fed breakfast upside down, I began throwing up not only my morning meal but also stomach bile. The bright green fluorescent discharge caught everyone's attention. I was immediately ushered out of the ICU for emergency surgery. I was helpless; my life was in the hands of strangers. I was being prepped; the charge nurse and other operating personnel explained that my stomach had perforated. My stomach exploded because of the stress and shock of the spinal cord injury and my body's inability to communicate sensations. They were going to cut me wide open, sew my stomach back together, and search for any other damage. The medical team transferred me onto the cold stainless steel slab and I could smell the overwhelming sterility of the air. My cognitive awareness slowly began to fade as the morphine and other sedatives had their way. My last clear recollection was a member of the surgical team cramming a G tube down the back of my throat to vacuum out the toxic waste that had exploded into my body.

My eyes peeled open to the same drab off-white ceiling tiles illuminated by the institutional fluorescent lights. I was in the exact same place that I was prior to the surgery. This time, however, my disposition was different.

I was now the proud owner of not one, but two, separate tubes. The first was the respirator helping me to breath and the second, the G-tube for feeding. Now, not only could I not move, but I couldn't speak or breathe on my own.

The ICU does not have days or nights, only shift changes and the nurses' life-sustaining activities. I was able to keep time by observing these shift changes. Every eight hours, a new nurse would attend to my needs, change my dressings and check my vital signs. The ICU is a relatively small room with a central nurses' station and five patient beds, two to the left and three to the right. I, possessing more injuries than others and therefore identified as having greater medical needs, occupied one of the nearest positions to the nurses' command station. The ICU does not permit family and friends to visit for extended periods of time. Instead, family and friends were only allowed approximately five minutes on every hour to visit their loved ones. In this regard, in case of emergency medical issues, which occur without warning, medical staff wouldn't have to navigate around family to provide treatment. This isolation away from family and friends, had a significant impact on my state of mind. Frequently, I would ask myself what I had done to deserve such physical and psychological pain. As I lay in bed, staring at the same drab ceiling tiles, there was no escaping or sharing the pain! I was in traction with screws in my head. Even without the traditional sense of feeling, paralysis does not inhibit the body from manifesting pain because my body was physically exhausted. Even though I was paralyzed, I still felt as if I had been run over by a truck. Pain must be expressed; the body learns new ways to communicate it. My blood pressure would rise, I would sweat, and my heart rate would race. Compounding the physical state was the inability to share all of these foreign sensations, I was trapped. I was so frustrated that I couldn't believe my entire body didn't explode.

Just when I thought I would be able to rest, one of the many unique noises made by the life support systems would wake me. Machines were pumping and beeping constantly. Being unable to move, talk, or feel, I could not ascertain whether this noise was my alarm, my body crashing, or someone else's. My only relief would come as the rushing of the nurses' feet raced past my bed to some other poor victim whose body could not withstand the pressures and stresses of his broken condition within the ICU.

The nurses and related therapists would attend to my daily regimen of physical therapy, body rotation, and blood work that occurred every three hours. Because I was unable to swallow and/or consume "real food," every 3-5 hours per day, a nurse would also take the plastic tube off my chest, insert a syringe full of white, milky nutrients, and shoot it up my nose. This medical milkshake launched up my nose constituted as my breakfast, lunch and dinner meals. During my incapacitated state, these regular milkshake treatments supplied intravenously would enable the necessary life-sustaining nutrients to feed my body for survival and healing.

Nearing one of my treatment sessions, my ears picked up on heavier footsteps on the floor. The new sound aroused my sense of sight and my eyes opened. To my surprise and relief, a Catholic priest was at the foot of my bed reading my chart. He was clearly concerned for my well-being; the history and the doctor's notes were not good.

He decided right then and there that I should be given the gift of the last rites. My relief turned into fear. I was seventeen; it wasn't my time to check out. I was unable to express my dismay because of the multiple tubes running down the back of my throat. My fear emanated from my eyes. The priest mistakenly interpreted my visual language for my running out of time. His reciting of the sacred and ancient prayer became more and more rapid along with my anxiety. The man of the cloth was unwittingly taking the one thing I needed: hope. I, too, was praying; only harder and faster than he was. The gods were listening; I didn't die.

3

After six weeks, I earned the privilege of being relocated from the ICU to a standard hospital room. It was pleasing to know that the medical experts no longer considered me on the verge of death. I was now on the miraculous road to recovery.

My first reward was a visit from my teammates. Before they entered the room, my mom thoroughly briefed them about what to expect in the hallway. She tried to explain what their friend, her son, had been through for the last six weeks, but words would not do it justice. As they all clambered into the 8x8 room, I mustered up as much enthusiasm as possible to demonstrate my latest achievement. Because I had limited mobility in my upper body, I mastered a clumsy and awkward flinging motion of my right forearm to my face. This was a shocking and grotesque action observed by my friends. They didn't know how to respond to their teammate who once bulldozed through the defensive line. Attempting to break the tension in the room, I jokingly, but very seriously, called out for help. "I haven't learned how to get my hand back down." It was warming yet painful to see my friends again. I knew for the first time how hard it was going to be to complete my mission. The way they looked at me is indescribable. It's more than shock and empathy. It was the same "unknown" expression I had seen earlier on my father's face. Their distance surrounded me, and the barrier between us was already built; little did I know that I would see the "unknown" look for the rest of my life.

My two football coaches appeared in the doorway, signaling my teammates to leave the room. The head coach took a place at the foot of the bed; the other pulled a chair up next to me. They began with words of comfort; neither of the gentlemen had experienced such an injury with one of his players before.

The coach closest to me began telling a story about a young 13-year-old freshman boy who stood six feet four and weighed over 200 pounds. He had surprising talent but absolutely no discipline. He did not appreciate history and culture of high school freshmen playing on the freshmen team. Halfway through the season, this young boy decided he had had enough and turned his back on the sport. Two years later, after acquiring two varsity letters in rowing and becoming competent at hockey, basketball, and all other sports, the young man decided to return to the football field his junior year during summer training. The coaches were unwelcoming; they did not want his attitude and undisciplined ways affecting their team. The much stronger, more confident, and more gifted adolescent stated that he was not going to waste his summer vacation on shenanigans. He authoritatively challenged the coaches for a chance to prove himself. Finally, at the end of the six weeks, this young man not only made the team but also the starting position as an offensive lineman.

Coach turned, looked me square in the eyes, and said, "That young man was you, JR. We have no idea what you have been through or what you will face in the future, but we are certain that should you choose to play to win, you will overcome this setback. The choice is yours."

It was then, at that moment, I decided that I was going to face the next stage of recovery, the rehab process, with the same zeal that I had for sports – play to win! I would listen to my coach this time and take his advice. I was not going to sit on the sidelines of life and wonder how far I could go; instead I was going to jump right into this strange and unfamiliar world of adaptive mobility head-on.

Unknowingly, I had been blessed by a decision my parents made. They chose to reject their military medical benefits complete with insurance and did not ship me off to the military rehab unit in Colorado. Instead, they chose to keep me in Chicago, one of the finest institutions at the time, and personally bear the financial repercussions of their decision.

On moving day, I was loaded on a gurney, and all of my worldly belongings were placed on my side: family pictures, a half dozen T-shirts, a couple of pairs of sweatpants, one pair of shoes, and a big box of get well cards. I was taken to the elevator, and with my mother by my side, we went to the basement. Traveling through the underground tunnel system to the adjoining rehab structure, I anxiously awaited my new beginning.

The Northwest Memorial Rehab Unit was humongous. It consisted of nine floors meeting the needs of a few hundred patients all requiring different rehab training. Some patients were quadriplegics like me; some were paraplegics; some were amputees; some had head injuries; and some were recovering from strokes. I found myself staring at them, wondering what had caused their injuries. We were divided by age and injury type.

I was directed to a floor, a room, and a bed. I shared this room with six other quadriplegics. My days started early at 6:00 a.m.; breakfast was at 7:00 a.m.; and therapies lasted from 8:00 a.m. to 3:00 p.m. daily. The only break in the regiment was one hour for lunch. Surprisingly, the routine made an awful lot of sense to me. It was almost like being back on campus because each day was broken into different sections and routines, all for a common cause.

I was assigned to both physical therapy and occupational therapy twice a day. I was required to have one session of psychological and vocational therapy daily as well. I was familiar with psychological therapy, but vocational training was preparing me for work experience. Basically, what was I going to do for work? What could I do?

My progress led up to my being able to enjoy a shower with hot running water every other day. This was a significant improvement from the occasional bed bath to maintain my hygiene. In the evenings on non-shower nights, I would receive tutoring for all of my high school classes. My six classes of personal maintenance during the day didn't compare to the difficulty of my academic studies. My father had arranged for a tutor and coordinated my studies to be consistent with my high school requirements. After all, if I were to graduate with my classmates, I had much work to catch up on. Nonetheless, it felt great to have a small sense of normality.

The rehab process is a regimented system to train the patient, and in some cases, family members to achieve adaptive and independent living skills. The first step of this long process for me was the fitting of a wheelchair. At this point, I had only occasionally sat in a loaner chair to practice some basic independent living skills. Because of the seriousness of my injuries, the only functional skills I had achieved at this point were sitting for a few hours at a time and my infamous arm flick.

I was still uneducated about the various nuances of paralysis, and my ego would not permit the rehab staff to fit me for one of the very ugly and archaic power wheelchairs. You see, even though my body no longer worked, my face, brain, and identity remained the same. I still wanted to be cool. A wheelchair becomes a part of a quadriplegics' attire; it reflects his/her personality. I actually remember lying on the gurney and stating emphatically, "I don't want one of those archaic, loud, mechanical power chairs!" I personally needed to know that I could manually push a chair instead of pushing a button forward. I needed to take an active role.

The medical technician, sensing my frustration, fetched not only the physical therapist but also the resident psychologist. In the end, we all agreed that although it would likely set my rehab back, they would allow me to work on the sport, manual wheelchair for a week. If at the end of the week I had not made progress, it would be a power chair from there on with no complaints or attitude. Remembering my coach's words "Play to win", and drawing upon my unrelenting tenacity, I was determined that they would not place me in a power chair.

After many hours of measuring and fine tuning, like being fitted for a tailor-made suit, I was placed into a sport wheelchair. Having only sat in a wheelchair for a short period of time and having no control over my stomach or chest muscles, I found even the simple act of balancing hard to handle. I also had no equilibrium, so the technicians decided to strap me into the chair to help me with my balance. I was ready mentally to propel the manual chair. Having only learned how to flap my arms around, actually pushing the chair would prove to be much harder than anticipated. As I raised both of my arms and engaged the tires, reality hit me hard in the face. No matter how hard I willed the chair to move, there I sat.

Every day after therapy, the nurses would place me in front of the TV to await the evening meal. Every day I would try to move the chair. My physical therapist put rubber tubing around the rims of the wheels and got some bike gloves for me hoping to increase the friction and grip. When that week ended, my persistence, hard work, and zeal to succeed actually paid off! I moved the wheelchair eight inches! As an athlete, it was the same feeling you get after making the play that wins the game.

This monumental achievement was empowering! It was my first step and I was learning to walk all over again. I was now free; I was now unshackled; I was no longer pushed around the hallways of the rehab. I did not have to look out the window, watch TV, or simply sit where I had been placed like a piece of furniture. I was free to come and go as I pleased. I had finally achieved a glimmer of independence, and a cool new manual, sport chair of my own was ordered for me.

4

I was now off the G-tube for feeding, and the occupational therapist arrived with an adaptive sling to facilitate self-feeding. The sling had a floor stand, springs, ace bandages, an elbow pocket, and a fork holder. It took the therapist 15 minutes to assemble the apparatus, place my right arm into the sling, and adjust the tension. After a several attempts the session was over, and the therapist left me strapped in for self-practice. As the door closed, the tears ran down my face. The only reasons I didn't throw the frick'n thing across the room were one, I physically couldn't, and two, I hated being fed by someone else even more. Therefore, day in and day out, I practiced shoveling. Once the ice cream softened to the point of melting, the nurse would come in and wipe my mouth, change my bib, and give me a new pint.

Eventually it all came together. At last, I was able to scoop the cold savoring reward into my mouth with continued success. I mastered the sling technique, range of motion, and balance. The following week, the therapist came in with a big box and a naughty smile.

"We are through with the sling and moving onto more dignified practices." she said.

"What's in the box?" I asked.

Without responding, she opened the case and there was an assortment of adaptive eating equipment. There were spoons, forks, plates, corn holders even a paperclip-like thing that would pinch a cheeseburger so I could hold it. I was curious, and it all looked "cooler" than the sling.

"This is going to be a journey," she said. "Trial by error."

So we started experimenting. I started with a big bowl and a non-slip place mat. Then we added a funny angled spoon and bib. I practiced with various food substances: cereal, soup, and, of course, JELL-O. Rehab's definition of independent drinking is sucking through a three-foot straw. Once again, my ego came into play, and I didn't want to look like an adult with a super-sized sippy cup. After burning my mouth on a cup of coffee through a straw, I had had enough and told my therapist to dig into her bag of adaptive tricks and find a replacement for the straw. We had to find a material and a cup that would stick to my wheel chair gloves and that would not require gripping. Would you believe, the perfect container turned out to be a 12-ounce Solo cup! It had a narrow base, and I could gently catch the top rim, wrap both my hands around it, and balance it carefully on my lips. One of the skills I mastered quite quickly was the "spill." I got tired of my crotch being either burned or wet, so I learned to throw liquids away from my body.

By the end of 100 different meals and spills, I gained the confidence and skills needed to eat my Thanksgiving dinner without assistance. Thanksgiving was made even more special because my family and I had learned enough about adaptive living to earn a four-hour pass to leave the rehab unit. My family learned about transfers, catheterizations, wheel chair adjustments, and anything that might happen or be required during the four hours. The first task on our adventure was attempting to get me into a car. The "transfer technique" isn't as easy as it sounds. It's not as simple as opening the door, lifting me out of the chair, and placing me into the seat. Someone had to first place the wheelchair parallel to the car door and then take the arms and leg rests off the wheelchair. Next, a sliding board had to be constructed. One end would go under my butt and the other onto the car seat. Then someone would slide me across the board and onto the seat. My legs would fold inside, and with a quick rotation, I was able to face forward. I was still wearing the cumbersome neck brace at the time. Therefore, my back and head had to angle so as not to hit the frame or roof of the car. Of course, my six-foot-five frame did not conveniently fit into a midsize car very well, and I was bumped, knocked, and scraped a few times.

After I was adjusted into my seat and facing forward, the wheelchair was folded and collapsed to fit into the trunk of the car. This whole procedure took almost 20 minutes. The rest of the family jumped into the car, and we drove to our cousins' house for dinner. I quietly reflected on how dangerous the Chicago highways and streets were. I was actually quite shocked about an everyday activity that never troubled me before. I was scared. It was the first time out of the safety of the hospital. The cars' swerving made me jump although I couldn't physically jump. The traffic lights seemed abrupt. I felt my blood pressure rise. My body started to spasm, and I could only assume that I was hyper sensitive to the vulnerability of my body and aware that I couldn't handle another trauma. Mr. "Cool" was not so cool after all.

After we arrived at our cousins' house, we began the 20-minute reversal process of getting me out of the car. Then came the front steps to the house. I had to be rolled backwards to go up approximately ten steps, bouncing along one step at a time just like the movers you see handling your furniture with a dolly. By the time we reached the front door, all the family had gathered, and I felt like I was the center ring in a three ring circus.

Once we were inside, my mother painstakingly removed the three layers of clothes I was wearing to handle the late November Chicago cold. Unwittingly, my family placed me in the hallway like a piece of furniture. The hugs, kisses, and questions came fast and furious. It was good to be out of the hospital for the first time in over 90 days. So much had changed; so much had happened, yet so much was still the same.

The chair I was in was not the one I had been using at the hospital; it was a loaner one that enabled me to go out. Therefore, I was not used to pushing or controlling it.

As friends and family enjoyed the merriment of the holiday, nobody saw my chair begin to creep forward. I slowly began to realize that I was picking up momentum and heading toward the basement stairs. In complete shock and just short of a basement tumble and another traumatic injury, I finally yelled out, "Mom!" The adults immediately stopped, realized what was happening, and caught me just in the nick of time. So much for having a simple and drama-free outing. My incident was a gentle reminder to all of us that things were always going to be different. As hard as we all might try to make things like they once were, they would never be the same. We had already used about two hours of our four-hour pass, so we all bellied up to the tables, gave thanks, and enjoyed one another's company. Adults sat at one table, children at another, and I had my first public meal pretty much unassisted. The only help I received was with the strapping on of my eating gizmo and slicing my turkey meat into bite size pieces. I was proud of myself; by the time dinner was over, I only had a little gravy on my hospital shirt and a few corn kernels scattered on the table, and I didn't take a face plant into the basement.

Having achieved some independent mobility and the capacity to self-feed, I found that my goal of getting back to school gained greater importance with each passing day. It was no longer some far-fetched ideal hope; it was real and attainable. At the end of each week, my mother could see measurable progress in my rehab. Each of my mother's weekend visits gave me the enthusiasm for the week to come and allowed my grandmother some time off in return. We were now training for a four-day pass to go home for Christmas. In order to receive the medical clearance, the whole family would have to learn more complex independent living skills including showering, bowel program, catheterization, stretching, dressing, and bed rotation. In addition, the family house had to undergo immediate modifications. The doorways and halls had to be widened; the bathroom had to be reconstructed; the kitchen table had to be elevated; and ramps had to be added. By the time Christmas came, everyone and the house had passed inspection. I had to be the expert on everything so I could coach others and be certain my care was correct. Because we had only four days, I flew home to Kentucky, not on a commercial jet, but on a small Sesna to save time. We thought getting in and out of the car had been a challenge; doing the "transfer technique" on to a plane deemed even more problematic. I was fortunate that my parents were still young, healthy, and strong enough to be able to lift and move me like a carefully-packaged Christmas gift. It took close to an hour to get me onto the airplane and another three hours of flying, but we finally landed in Kentucky. It was good to be home, to be able to lie in my own bed, and to see the family dog. It's amazing how your pets never forget and always love. How life had changed, though. Everything centered on me. What time would I get up, how would I get to church, and what did I want for dinner? Everyone was on pins and needles, and I was this fragile doll they were afraid to break. It was clear that a spinal cord injury had a devastating and lasting effect, not only on me, but also on the whole family. My parents and brother were now my nurses and caregivers. I couldn't get something to eat; I couldn't walk the dog. My capacity to contribute to the home had been taken away, and now I was another chore on the list. I couldn't set the table, take out the garbage, or dress the Christmas tree. All I could do was sit there and watch. They continually asked me what I needed, and I would think to myself, *If I need anything I'll let you know!* Each family member, including my brother, would take turns addressing my four-times-daily personal needs. Mom did most of the hands-on activities throughout the day, and my Dad and brother would do most of the lifting. On our first night, amazingly, everything went seamlessly. The next morning, we realized everything didn't quite go as planned. Unfortunately, I awoke with the bed soaked in my own urine. It happened because Dad had plugged the night bag into the condom catheter without taking the cap off the night bag. While I was getting cleaned, Mom explained to Dad how the night bag and condom catheter should really work. Of course he took this criticism in stride, but I was the one swimming in urine. I realized that I had to pay more attention to my care giving if I did not want to sleep in urine again. Once I was dressed, my mother ran to the store to purchase one of those plastic mattress pads. This was the first of many "caregiver quadriplegic" solutions, (which I have termed *MacGyver tricks)*, that my family, caregivers and I would have to invent over the years.

Because I had not yet personally reconciled my feelings about the injury, I would from time to time lash out at those around me. Like most families, we have our routine and traditions. Once everyone was awake, we would open stockings. For the first time in 17 years, I didn't just stumble out of bed and tear open my stocking. The morning routine had to start with a catheterization, bowel program, leg therapy, bathing, dressing, and morning medicine. During this two-hour routine, my brother and father had walked the dog four times, checked on my progress several times, and made their own tire tracks in the carpet awaiting my arrival. Presents for the Harding's historically had a functional application behind them. Mom wrapped my presents in cloth material and scotch tape, a consideration that I thought was brilliant. This wrapping technique allowed me to fumble with each present but still open them independently. It was both empowering and very frustrating. In some cases, it took up to ten minutes for me to open one present... while everyone was watching, of course. At this point in my therapy, my arm dexterity and wrist function were the primary focus of my physical therapy. My father told me how he had thought long and hard about a practical and functional present for weeks. After I fumbled about with the heavy box for what seemed an eternity, out slid the gift. They were the new cool hand-held jogging weights. I was dumbfounded. While I understood his intent, my father missed the mark completely. My hands did not work; I could not hold the weights, and therefore they were junk. Coupled with my own disability anger, I could not fake my enthusiasm for the gift.

I said something like, "You don't get it! You never asked."

My father, who was not used to being wrong and certainly not accustomed to his son's criticism, promptly got up from the Christmas tree and walked away.

My brother turned to me… "You did it this time! You ruined Christmas!" Then he stormed out of the room.

There my mother and I sat with the family broken. I was not free to roll off into another room like the others. I was stuck feeling awkward. What I did not fully understand at the time of the gift opening was how hard my father had struggled over an appropriate gift to give his now quadriplegic son. According to my mother, he had spent days trying to find the "right" present, and with absolutely no positive recognition from me for his efforts, he was hurt greatly. He wanted to embrace my optimism, join me in physical therapy, and share my advances, and I instead cut him off at the knees. In a way, we had all been pretending. We knew things would be different, but in reality, we didn't know how different our lives would be. I was not the same. Never would be. The trials of quadriplegia now put a strain on all of us.

The next day the family gathered my gear except for the weights my father had given me and returned me to the rehab hospital. I was thankful to return to a safe environment built for my issues. They knew what I could and could not do there. They understood my needs without me having to tell them. I learned several important lessons over the holidays. My family members could support me, love me, and guide me but should not be my care providers. I couldn't expect them to know what I was going through or anticipate my every need. They were learning with me. We were going to have to stumble through this together, yet separately. I had so much personal bullshit to deal with, and it was starting to come out. I needed to keep my emotions under control. I knew I still had a lot to learn and come to terms with.

Monday morning arrived, and I was back at it. I was diving into new territory: hydrotherapy. Water is an environment that would allow me more ability to move and free me from the barriers of gravity. Therefore, my neck brace had to come off. I had been in the brace for three months, and it had become a part of my daily life. It controlled my range of motion, how I turned, and all of my robotic movement. The only time I had experienced a free neck was during the every-other-night shower program. While laying on the padded gurney in the shower, the rehab tech would carefully remove the neck brace for cleaning while I lay motionless.

The graphing of my shin bone to my spinal cord was successful, and now the doctor was going to remove my brace permanently. As I was sitting in the chair; he took it off, removed the shackle, and told me to turn my head. I was petrified and was afraid to move. It was as if my training wheels had just been taken off my ten speed bicycle. I no longer had the safety surrounding my neck. I was horrified because I hadn't realized my dependency on the brace. Finally, he convinced me to slowly turn my head left and right and up and down and thus let go of my security blanket. I immediately realized the limited range of movement the doctor's had warned me about.

I was stoked about getting into the pool and had fond memories of being on the swim team and serving as a life guard. Now, I would no longer dive into the pool, but a large crane, like a forklift, would pick me up and gently lower me into the pool. In the water, I had mobility and range of motion that were beyond my capacity of sitting in a chair. I felt weightless and free. In reality, I had lost the ability to tread water, flip, and otherwise keep my head above water. Therefore, I needed constant supervision. Nevertheless, it was fun to explore a new domain and to feel the warmth of the water around me. It always seemed as though time was up as soon as I got comfortable, and I would be hoisted right back into the cold air and placed back into my wheelchair.

I can't imagine the fear that must have passed through other paralyzed patients whose spinal cords had been broken in the water and who laid there drowning until their friends or someone else rescued them. What a horrible experience it must have been.

Building independence was a critical function to the rehab process. Once healthy enough and confident with our mobility device (manual or power chair), the rehab team would take us on regular field trips into the real world. In this case, the real world did not have flat hallways, ramps at 1 and 12, power doors, and simple sensitivity for the adaptive population. Outings were granted to small groups each week. We would visit McDonalds, the famous Chicago Giordanos' Pizzeria, the mall, museums, and the bonus trip - the Police Synchronicity concert, which was the best outing of them all, and due to arrive a week after my discharge. Since I had spent nearly six months of my life in rehab, I had earned the right to go to the Police show. With a little help from my therapists, and some good old JR charm, we collectively extended my stay by inventing a few new milestones for me to achieve, make the show and thus purchasing the time from the insurance company.

The Police Synchronicity Concert was a big deal in February of 1984. Everyone in rehab wanted to go, but there was only room for twelve of us. Naturally, I ended up with one of the limited seats. All of my friends knew I would be at the concert. I do not know what was better, the musical performance or meeting up with a dozen friends. Many of these friends could not make it to the hospital for a visit, but a Police show was one of those community calendar events. This time with my friends was well-spent. We laughed and drank during the entire concert. Of course, the therapist became very upset with me. Perhaps it was because every time she checked in on me I had a new beer.

Although I didn't appreciate it at the time, the concert and seeing my friends again turned my perspective around. "Roxanne...you don't have to put on the red light!" I began to realize so many things about my situation that comforted me. I was really fortunate in so many ways. What a joke, here I was severely paralyzed and yet grateful. I saw so many others who were worse off than me, and it gave me strength to persevere.

Discharge day was approaching fast, and so much was happening. I crammed in my studies; my own adaptive equipment was beginning to arrive; my family members had passed their tests; and insurance and medical papers were signed. I was not the only one starting to get emotional about leaving. The nurses and doctors had become a surrogate family, and I was going to miss them. We had shared birthdays, tears, and monumental strides. While showering one night, one of my nurses was telling me how much she was going to miss my beautiful smile, sparkling eyes, and enthusiasm.

"What ya gonna do when ya get out of here?" she asked.

"I'm going to take a shower every day. If I can't have a shower every day, leave me here."

I looked forward to making my own rehab rules and schedule. I looked forward to being the one in control of my body and its needs. They had done all they could for me, and now it was up to me to take what they had taught me and get myself back into the game of life.

5

I t was time to stand on my own again, so to speak. Since the injury, I had actually gained quite a sense of humor about my disability. I find it puts people more at ease. The day had finally come to return to my high school. My family, the community, and the school had been preparing for my return for a number of weeks. The school was over 200 years old and lacked any sense of accessibility. This was well before the passing of the Americans with Disabilities Act (ADA), and they didn't have to allow me to return, nor were they required to abide by any rules or laws to provide accessibility because it was a private institution. The red brick ivy buildings were adorned with stairs, so the administration had to identify all my classes and relocate them to the first floor of buildings with simple ramp mechanisms. They even fitted the mess hall with a 120 ft. ramp to overcome the 50 stairs going into the building. Dave, my roommate for the past two years, didn't have to pack up and move with me, but he did. He was willing to sacrifice a corner room on the third floor (with two windows) for a first-floor room next to the noisy group bathroom. I'm not sure that I would have done the same. I was grateful. His friendship and dedication right from the start helped me to integrate back into the school environment that I had so longed for. Everyone had gone out of their way for me. My parents, with the school's assistance, found a volunteer firefighter-EMT to serve as my primary personal care assistant. I needed four treatments per day (morning, noon, afternoon, and night). The school's sports trainer, Tye, who used to prepare my ankles and wrists for football, would assist with a catheterization after his obligations were done with the varsity team in the afternoons. I just needed to get there.

As an extreme extravert, I get my strength from being around people, and I couldn't wait to return to my friends. My parents drove me from Kentucky trailing a U-Haul. It was not your typical boarding school trunk with clothing and accessories. Instead I was taking new tools for survival. The trailer was packed full of medical supplies, a power chair (I submitted to using power at times), a shower chair, a hospital medical bed, egg crates, and much more. Because I now sat at 160 pounds versus my previous weight of 220 lbs., I had to be fitted for new uniforms, so it was almost like starting my freshman year all over. A pressure sore on my foot prevented me from wearing the hard-soled shoes which were part of the cadet military uniform. Because I am unable to move most of my body, the skin suffocates and results in sores. Pressure sores can occur anywhere at any time on the body. Pressure sores and bladder infections are the two most common ailments that individuals with paralysis face. Although I was trained and educated about them in the hospital, each time it's unpredictable, scary, and mostly annoying for me because it takes so long for both of them to recover and heal.

I was excused from daily room and uniform inspections. Needless to say, I no longer marched or had to appear for ranks or drill. While rehabbing at the hospital, I had drawn from my memories of the good times, being a part of the team, leading my friends productively and unproductively. It became quite clear that no matter how hard I would try, I would never completely fit back in to Culver as I knew it.

The faculty was very patient and accommodating, which surprised me because I had not earned their favor in the past. Most of my friends didn't know what to do; each would get his courage up individually to come and say hello. None of them had experienced a friend or an acquaintance in a wheelchair before. In their eyes, I looked sickly. I was no longer the six-foot jock. I was now a skinny, frail guy in a wheelchair with awkward movements. I had a different schedule from everyone else. My adaptive way of life controlled my schedule. I was unable to row at 6:00 a.m. with the first boat varsity, stroll through the mess hall, or play ultimate Frisbee. When I did try to join in, I was welcomed, but it was clumsy. Everyone was nervous. They would ease a bit when I smiled and talked to them as I usually would. Everyone would always finish the conversation with, "Anything I can do?" I think they wanted something they could do for me. I think it was their way of making me feel welcome. Interestingly, the underclassmen seemed to be more at ease with me. Maybe I was more approachable to them now because they hadn't known me before the accident.

The biggest obstacle for the upper classmen with my return appeared to be the relationship between me and my offenders. Truthfully, I was uncomfortable and nervous about seeing Hawk and Jake again. The last time I had seen those two was the night of September 25, 1983, when my teammates, my classmates, my co-captains taught me a lesson about adolescent consequences. Did I hate them? No. Were they my friends? Not really. But the event was unavoidable; I was going to have to face them eventually. The campus was not big enough to avoid each other. We all tried. None of us wanted to face the night and action that could never be taken back.

I don't remember exactly when- maybe I blocked this out as well – but Jake initiated a conversation with me between classes. He said he wanted to talk. He wanted to know how I felt and to apologize for his actions. I reluctantly agreed, and we met later that night in the senior building. It was one of the most awkward moments in my life. Part of me wanted to spit in his face, shoot him in the head, and frankly just cuss him out. When I rolled up to the table, I could tell he was equally uncomfortable, but I had to give him credit for reaching out. I didn't snap, yell, or roll over him with my wheelchair.

"How are you?" He asked.

"How do you think?" I replied.

"I have no idea." Jake commented.

He really wanted to know the ins and outs of my injury and was truly curious, but I just didn't want to let him in. I think he understood.

He apologized for both he and Hawk, and I let it be.

As time passed, I never chatted with Hawk. He never apologized. Would I apologize to someone who I permanently injured? I don't know. I would hope so. On occasion we would make eye contact, but neither of us made the move to communicate.

I eventually saw Lori, my now-former girlfriend. She was happy I was back. She had cried for me months ago but had soon forgotten and moved on to another cadet and moved on with her life. At first, I would eat alone in the mess hall, but slowly people started to join me.

The winter weather broke, and it was spring. Campus life returned to its normal way, and many of my Culver memories returned. Frisbees were flying; lacrosse balls were thrown, and the co-eds were sunbathing in the greens. I was bombarded with memories that were now not adding up. I was not out rowing on the lake or playing pick-up intramural softball on the open green fields overlooking the lake. Instead, I was sitting on the sidelines in a chair. I was watching, no longer taking an active role in life; I was breaking the promise I made myself in the hospital after hearing my coaches' words of encouragement. With the help of some of my friends, we invented things for me to do. We created my own new work out program. I would push down the recreation department's long hallways. Then we added some weights to my routine by strapping them to my forearms. In a matter of weeks, we had established my "active" lifestyle. The girls started to walk with me; they even started to carry their own individual weights. They became my cheerleaders and a part of my new team. I was a jock of sorts again.

I was also learning to ask for help and not feel guilty about it. I began teaching others about my disability and how to handle me in case of emergencies. I realized that the more people knew about me and my adaptive needs, the more freedom and choices I had.

Freedom of choice comes with consequences. The one common denominator that wasn't removed because of my disability was that I was still able to get into trouble just like everyone else. Two weeks before graduation, it was customary for recent graduates to return to campus and help others celebrate their achievements. One Friday evening when I was already down for the night, I heard a knock on my window. Since I was unable to answer it myself, Dave went to the window to see what was up.

Ron from the class of '83 grinned from outside the window and said, "Let me in; it's Miller time!"

Three cases of beer came through the window with him. I immediately told Dave, my partner in crime, to get me out of bed. I felt that same "being bad" adrenaline pumping through my veins again, and I loved it. Somewhere around 12:30 a.m., we were drunk, and miraculously, my EMT aide reappeared. Recklessly, the four of us rolled me out the front door of the barracks and into the pickup truck. Off we went to the golf course to go 4-running. After our second pass around the nine holes yelling and screaming, we were greeted by the entire county police force.

To be honest, nobody really knew what to do. We were caught red handed, and then there was me. We were loaded up and taken to the school's infirmary for detox. The EMT was fired for his part in the incident. By all accounts, we should have been expelled on the spot. Instead, everyone looked the other way because of my quadriplegia. Our senior privileges and our rank were removed. We were put on restriction, but we were not kicked out of school, and we could still graduate. I quickly realized that in fact, there was some added special value to my circumstance. I was always good at pushing the boundaries, but now I was able to push the boundaries in a different way and the system was adapting with me.

Even though my friends and I were on restriction, the days were passing quickly. I couldn't get enough interaction with my old and new friends. It was simply fabulous to be a part of the campus life again. I had spent three and half years at Culver, and now it was my turn to graduate. Graduation is considered the sign of passing through adolescence into adulthood, and I had truly experienced much that year. I had grown in ways no 17-year-old should ever have to. I awoke the morning of graduation with a different adrenaline pumping. My normal two-hour morning routine seemed to take forever. The seniors were briefed on the program and details of the day: which uniform to wear, where we would line up, and where our friends and family could observe. The *Dress A* uniform fell flat against me, and the white waist belt didn't do justice to a person sitting in a wheel chair, but I didn't care. I looked down at my tennis shoes instead of the black-soled shoes and shrugged. Nothing was going to ruin this day. We lined up alphabetically between the troop and battery barracks. We marched symbolically through the archway past the flag pole, down the street, and then on to the parade field. I rolled while everyone marched in step. I was stuck between John L. Green III and the Harlan twins. They were not very graceful lifting me over the sidewalk. We were heading north toward the lake. The divots in the grass caused me to fall forward in the power wheel chair. Not having stomach or back muscles, I couldn't bring myself back to the upright position while simultaneously driving the chair. I did not want to make a scene, so I kept marching forward with my head between my knees.

I heard Ralph scream, "Sit him up! Sit him up!"

The H's surrounding me were clueless. The drums were beating, and we kept marching forward.

My good friend and fellow teammate George broke ranks; he was an M, so he came from the back of the line running, grabbed me by my navy blue jacket, and sat me up. "Come on, man, this is our big day. Don't blow it!"

Once we were lined up and ready for the procession, one of the administrators took an underclassman and assigned him to me, relieving George of his friendly duties. The speeches began – the traditional "You've come this far, you have an obligation to take your place in the world with pride in your strength and character...." The co-eds in their pretty white dresses went first. Although there were only about 65 girls, it seemed to take forever. Then it was time for the cadets. They began to read the names: John Albritton III, Don Anderson, Mike Blum... All I could think about was not falling over again. I didn't want to be that kind of spectacle; I wanted people staring for different reasons. I had that strength and character they referred to in the speech, and I didn't want my head in between my knees. As my name was read, James Raymond Harding II, I began to cry. I could see my father standing on the other side of the gate in his *Class A* uniform. As I moved forward, I said to the freshman, "Don't you dare come out there with me!" He was smart and let me have a head start before following behind. He was far enough back that he was not in my space or taking away from my independence. As I rolled closer to the superintendent, I was overwhelmed with emotion. As I passed through the gate, I saw my father beaming with pride because this was his goal, too. I had no idea how many faculty and staff members and friends watched my every move. They gazed in amazement, tears rolling down their cheeks as they cheered me on. I received a standing ovation from family, friends, and strangers alike. It was better than winning any football game...ever. Soon, all the cadets had passed through the arch, and the ceremonial hats flew into the air. And as the hats dropped to the ground, I realized that my entire being had centered on graduating with my class. Now what was I going to do?

6

I decided to go to Western Kentucky University so that I could continue my education. It was a state college; some of my hometown friends were attending; and it fell under section 504 of the Rehab Act (which required public universities receiving federal money to accommodate persons with disabilities). Therefore, attending a public university near my parents' home facilitated the possibility of emergency interventions should they be necessary. This was a big step as I had only been in a wheelchair for less than a year. I really didn't know what I could and couldn't do. I was seventeen and still learning about life with a significant disability and all that went with it. I did know one thing very clearly; that was, the Harding boys were expected to go to college. They were expected to learn, they were expected to graduate, and they would be independent, self-sufficient and contribute to the community.

I moved into a jock dorm, mostly because it was the dormitory closest to all the academic buildings and the easiest one for the university to make functionally accessible. The university was nervous because they never had to accommodate someone with my level of needs before. They installed a roll-in shower, multiple ramps, automated doors, and so forth. I had my own private shower, so I didn't have to share the community shower with everyone else, and I had some level of privacy for my adaptive and facilitated hygiene practices. On day one, with a brand new bathroom, with special doors, and with all of the attention I was receiving, it was very clear that I was their first student with a significant disability. I was their guinea pig.

While the university was required to provide me with academic accommodations and some physical accommodations, I was required to cover, recruit, and manage my personal care needs. With my parents' help, I recruited a fellow freshman working his way through college to serve as my primary assistant Monday through Friday. I also found a retired auto mechanic to serve as my weekend assistant. Having two personal care assistants was critical. As I had learned firsthand in 1983 with my injury, the gods have a way of adding obstacles into everyone's lives. Therefore, no matter what happened to one of my aides in his personal life, I always had a way to get in and out of bed and to meet my related daily medical needs.

The campus bus/shuttle did not have wheelchair lifts, and the most common travel was walking or bicycling. The university, working in concert with the student affairs director, organized my schedule and the location of my classes to be a convenient distance from my dormitory. I was grateful for the accommodations because the university was nicknamed "the hill toppers." Although there are no true mountains in Bowling Green, Kentucky, the campus was spread across a 10,000 yard hill. My power chair could only handle one trip up the hill per day. Therefore, I started my classes at the top of the hill and worked my way back down during the course of the day.

Late into the first semester, one of the student journalists chose to do a profile on me – a huge human interest story. The university had a real person with a real significant disability attending their school. They made a big to-do and gloated about making all necessary and appropriate changes to accommodate me. However, I just wanted to be a normal college kid; I didn't want the attention. Everybody was in my business. I had absolutely no privacy. Students were assigned to assist me with getting through doors, eating, and taking notes in class. Due to the lack of quality accessibility throughout campus, I frequently fell out of my wheelchair or fell off the curb and nearly everyone on campus knew how to put me back in my wheelchair. Once again, everyone wanted to make sure I was OK.

Since everyone was always in my business, all I wanted to do was escape. I turned to the pot smokers. These fellow students, some jocks, some hippies, and some just everyday students understood privacy and the need for secrets! They couldn't care less about my disability and accepted me for who I was. Or so I thought. Those who were officially assigned to me by the university didn't know how to handle my pot smoking. It wasn't like I could hide it from anyone. I couldn't quite sneak into the john and light myself a quick joint. I had to ask to have the bong filled, lit, and even put to my mouth. Shit, the only thing I could do on my own was inhale and exhale. My whole life was facilitated by friends and family.

Honestly, getting high was easier than dealing with my feelings. It's impossible to express what it is like to have your independence, your freedom, and your decision-making shared with others. It had been barely a year since I was the star player, the one you always wanted on the team, the one who always had to go somewhere at 3:30 in the afternoon, be it practice or the Friday night game! I found myself sitting on the sidelines. I had no purpose. I could no longer partake in my passion for sports. I no longer had personal goals. I was simply wandering through the college environment of frat parties, girls, and occasional academics. I had discovered that I had way too much time on my hands. We all know the saying, "Idle hands make for the Devil's time." In the past, all my time had been managed for me. Now, just 18, as a young adult, I had no experience with self-determination and appropriate time management.

By the middle of the second semester, the administration was on their last nerve. The numerous reports from the RA and the dorm director with regard to my shenanigans had begun to occupy too much of their time. They wanted me to succeed as a student, the DISABLED student, but they were also not willing to tolerate or take a chance of my delinquent behavior backfiring. My risky behavior wasn't just limited to pot smoking and college drinking but also included a violation of the coed rules. All females had to be removed from the building by 10:00 p.m. I continually broke the 10:00 p.m. rule and kept pushing the limits.

A classmate from Culver came to visit in his 1979 yellow Camaro in the late spring of '85. I wanted to show off and prove to him that I had adjusted to college life and really fit in. The best way to crowd a room and look popular was to provide free alcohol. I remember watching him slyly roll a keg covered with blankets into the room. The funny thing was we really did think we were smart and concealed our pre-party activities. It didn't take long for the blaring Led Zeppelin, the continuous flow of people, and the smell of alcohol to catch the eye of the RA. He busted up the party and indicated that this was the last straw. My blatant disregard for the rules had finally forced him to take action. He could no longer look the other way.

The next morning, hung-over and embarrassed in front of my friend, I was summoned to the office of the Vice-President of Student Affairs. He felt he could no longer manage "the JR risk."

"Due to continuous neglect for the campus rules, I have to ask you to move off campus." He said.

Of course, I thought I could bat my pretty blue eyes and get out of it, convince him to take yet another chance on me.

"JR, the liability is too great. Instead of kicking you out this very minute, I've decided that you can continue your education with us, but you will have to do so off campus. Don't push it!"

I was more than happy to move off campus. I could choose my roommates and engage in illicit activities without the fear of being caught or reprimanded by the school administrators. The best part was that I wouldn't have to check the girls in and out; they could simply spend the night.

Five of us found a ratty old house just off campus and modified it by building a ramp and fixing the bathroom. "Modifications," is an understatement. The ramp we built was so steep that someone had to walk me up and down it; the bathroom included widening the doors; and there was no roll-in shower. But my friends and I made it work.

All in all, I thought it was cool. It was the first time I was actually living with others, real people, not nurses or prescribed individuals to assist me, just everyday college kids. Life was good; I was getting by on social security, help from my parents, partaking in illicit activities, and, once again, just doing enough in school to get by.

Ironically or perhaps planned behind the scenes for my benefit, my family took a trip to Ohio and looked into Wright State University in Dayton. The school was selling me on all the barriers that had been removed and prided themselves on integration. They had a wheelchair basketball team, scientific experiments with electrical stimulation going on, underground tunnels that connected all the classrooms and dormitories, electric doors, and more. I was surrounded by a cloud of guilt when I was with my family. I knew, and they knew, that I had not been living up to their expectations. Because of the pressure from my family and their concern for my current situation, I reluctantly realized that I should transfer to Wright State. Part of me was excited, but mostly I was scared that I wouldn't fit in because I didn't know a soul. My family would be almost five hundred miles away, and I no longer would be the only disabled student on campus. I would become just one of many students with a disability.

Accessible on-campus housing was hard to get; rooms were a premium. Vans would leave campus to pick up students with disabilities and take us to campus as their way of accommodating us. I had a total of 17 credits transferred out of a possible 30. When I arrived at Wright State in the fall of 1985, I was basically starting my freshman year over.

Because I was a summer transfer student, there was no way I was getting the premium on campus housing. I was both fortunate and unfortunate to cut a business deal with an upper classman. He was an experienced personal care assistant and needed a roommate. I covered the rent and food, and he, in turn, took care of me. Both of my essential needs were met. Because he was a random roommate and we had no experience together, we quickly realized we were not a good match. We were completely different. He did not appreciate my friends or activities. He had a controlling personality that sometimes resembled a character from the horror movie, *Misery*. One morning, instead of waking me, getting me showered and dressed, and sending me off to class, he announced that he could no longer work for me. He walked out of my bedroom, smiled and shut the door. I was so pissed at myself thinking I could get by with just one aide. I was stranded. The situation was surreal. What was I going to do? I had developed the habit of keeping the phone next to me for emergencies, which was another MacGyver trick I learned. I called the operator by using my tongue. Back then real people actually answered the phone. I explained the situation, and she offered to call the police. I said, "No, please call my girlfriend." Even though we'd only been dating for a couple of months, Mindy came right over.

Mindy had to crawl in through the window because I was unable to open the door. While I was still lying in bed she asked, "So now what are we going to do?" Honestly, I had no idea, but I tried to remain optimistic. Mindy was unable to get me in and out of the bed or the wheelchair. She could, however, handle all of my daily needs. I suggested that we ask the soldiers who lived above me to help. They agreed and for the next week, every morning and night, they would do the lifting, and Mindy would do the care. During this time, I was unable to focus on school but instead worried about where was I going to live and who was going to take care of me.

I was in luck; a freshman with a disability occupying an on-campus dorm room had gone home. He had given up and thrown in the towel, leaving his college ambitions behind. The university, being extremely accommodating for its 1,500 students with disabilities, notified me of the vacancy. I couldn't believe my luck. My handful of new friends and Mindy relocated me over the weekend onto campus. By the end of the week, I had completely moved out, signed all the paperwork, and recruited two new personal care assistants. The gods were clearly smiling upon me. In actuality, I had handled the crisis all on my own.

The campus dorm showers had six handicapped stalls.

The disabled were lined up six in a row, with room for six aides. The able bodies would come into the showers stunned to have to walk around six different shower chairs. Many of them had not seen or experienced people with disabilities, let alone showered with six of us. I, too, was adjusting to being with others with significant disabilities. I was soberly reminded that I was blessed because I could be worse. I would look around the dining hall and see the girl with no arms or legs and the guy on the ventilator. I felt better because they were smiling, beating each other in chess and enjoying life. I was no longer "special"; I was one of many. I now felt like a normal college student.

During my years at Wright State, my friends and I became exceptionally good at pushing our boundaries. It was not so much breaking the rules but making access when there were no guidelines, standards or other public policy. One of my more colorful stories included a trip to the Grateful Dead concert at the Cincinnati River Front. Yes, attending a Grateful Dead concert means everything – drugs, sex, and rock n' roll. In this particular case, my friends and I rented a yellow school bus equipped with two kegs of beer so nobody would have difficulties getting back and forth to the concert. We were able to park the big yellow school bus in the handicapped parking space right in front of the arena. All my friends, and some I barely knew, stumbled out of the big yellow bus, and I had to be carried off. Everyone was searched going through security, but I rolled right on in with my book bag filled with booze.

In the fall of 1989, I was sitting in my on-campus apartment planning how to finish my senior year, when they knocked at my door.

"Mr. Harding..." another knock at the door. "This is the police. Open this door immediately." They demanded.

I was stone cold and curious. I slowly rolled towards the door. "I'm coming." I responded.

They didn't hear me and opened the door. They were obviously shocked to see a handsome, blue eyed charmer in a wheelchair.

"I was trying..." I said as they entered.

The policeman looked stunned. "Sorry kid- but you need to come downtown to the station."

"Yah, what for? Not rolling to the door faster?" I said sarcastically.

"No, kid – your so-called friend ratted you out. You're busted." My body had muscles spasms all the time, but I don't think I have ever trembled like that before in my entire life.

I couldn't believe that one of my pot smoking friends had sold me out to the police. So there I was, five days before I turned 21 and a semester before graduation, and I was now faced with the possibility of jail.

Had I not been in serious trouble, I would have felt the next episodes funny. They'd hoped to take me away in the paddy wagon. After wheeling me down the steepest and ricketiest ramp, there was this nice big wagon and both of the police officers looked at each other when we rolled up next to the vehicle. It was not accessible. So they commandeered a school bus which had a lift to take me to the courthouse. I was terrified and I felt alone.

I thought, "Now I've really done it. I'm not a criminal; I'm not a bad person; but I'm being taken to jail." It was the longest ride, the quietest ride, and most dreadful trip in a vehicle I have ever taken. I noticed while riding that the rest of the world just continued doing what it was doing without knowledge and/or concern of how my world was falling apart.

Once off the school bus, I couldn't get into the jail cell, so they had to create a temporary holding spot until the judge provided further direction. They brought me through the back door and the kitchen service area. The inmates in the kitchen looked at me funny because I was being guarded by the sergeant. They were thinking I must've done something really, really wrong to have a sergeant guarding me. Then they took me to intake to begin my paperwork.

Name: JR Harding. The sergeant filled in it.

Address: I dictated.

"Can you read?" and the cop laughed at himself. "Yah, but he's just a bit stupid," and winked at me.

He reiterated my stupid behavior and how this particular judge liked making examples out of college students. The judge was mad; he had been disturbed over the weekend and bothered with an idiotic college kid problem. He did not want to treat me any differently than the other college students he taught lessons to. But he knew and I knew that I wasn't spending the night because the local jail wasn't accessible, and I had personal care needs that needed to be attended to. Like it or not, I was already getting special treatment. I wanted this over as quickly as possible, so I admitted under a plea bargain that I knowingly distributed illegal substances. He gave me three years' probation; 500 hours of community service; and a fine of $5,000.00. I would not be released from probation until the fine and the community service hours were completed. So they released me but did not take me home. There I was sitting outside the police station all alone and with no way to get home. Talk about being thrown to the curb.

Sitting on the lonely curb on a sunny afternoon, with my life and freedom in complete disarray, I had to flag down a complete stranger. I needed to find a payphone and get help making a call to my personal care assistant. Fortunately he was home and waiting for an update, he quickly came to my rescue.

The university suspended me for a year. The dean was pissed.

"JR, you are the worst student problem I have had to contend with. Coupled with your special needs, it makes it even more difficult because I have to treat you equally. You have 24 hours to vacate the property."

I made the headlines again: "Handicapped Student Arrested."

I was certain that my parent's displeasure would be significant. I had my aide press down the record button on my tape recorder so I could record a message... *"Mom and Dad, JR here. I know you are busy in Germany, but I kind of have some disappointing news for you."* I mailed them a tape. Yes, I frickin' mailed them a tape explaining my ordeal. I couldn't bring myself to hear the frustration and anger in my father's voice.

I spent the first 48 hours in a hotel, and then I found an off-campus apartment less than 300 yards away from the university on the ground floor. In less than 3 days, I managed to sign a lease, relocate, and keep a roof over my head. I was getting pretty good at this. While my basic needs had been met, I was lost as to my direction and purpose. Worse, now I couldn't even call myself a student.

Finding myself in the pits of hell, alone and lost, I decided to reach out for help. For the first time in my life, I turned to authority figures for assistance. I turned to one of my professors who referred me to a colleague who had just received a federal grant toward disabled rehabilitation. I was to be a guinea pig again. Any other person looking for help or gaming the system could find resources within his own community, but I had to go to Minnesota for treatment. It was the only residential program within 500 miles that could accommodate a quad. I was going not because I thought I needed help, but because I finagled the court system to allow me to apply this time toward my community service hours. I was completely shocked by the many professionals who came to get their lives back on track. Every profession imaginable: doctors, lawyers, policemen... and then there was me. We were learning to balance addiction – something we all had in common in our lives. The program director knew that I was using the 30 days to satisfy community service hours, so he forced me to be honest in the sessions, in my journaling, and with myself. I humbly earned my certificate, completed my 30 days, and was "re-habbed." Even though I entered the program to game the system, I ended up gaming myself, and I landed on a new path.

Once back in Ohio, I turned to the university faculty again for their assistance and leadership. I was able to get back into school for the spring semester on a probationary period. The 18 hours of class work and the abuse aftercare program kept me out of trouble. I didn't have time to misbehave. Slowly, the principles of the recovery program began to have a positive effect on me. The only thing I had to do was change and change everything. I no longer hung out with the pot smokers; I focused on studying and discovered that I could actually apply myself. I found myself advocating for accessibility throughout the campus. In the summer of 1991, I graduated from college and had been accepted to a graduate school in Pensacola, Florida.

Relocating to Pensacola, Florida, was the fourth time I had completely uprooted my adaptive way of life. Moving for anyone is not easy, but moving with a significant disability offers more challenges. I needed to live near accessible public transportation. I needed a roll-in shower, and I needed to be able to recruit people to assist with my various care taking needs. The easiest place for my success would be on campus. It was a world I had become familiar with. It was the one environment I understood. The University of West Florida, a smaller school, was perfect for my needs. The town was conservative and convenient. Night life was not as plentiful as it could have been in other parts of the country, including the one I had just left. I knew I was there as a courtesy; the faculty at Wright State fought hard to get the graduate faculty to take a chance on me. I had been given a second chance, and I knew I needed to make the best of it.

7

My father decided he would visit me for the Thanksgiving holiday and examine my new life at West Florida. This get-together was like a re-birth or a renewal for my father and me. The last time we had spoken, I had fallen off the Harding path. I hadn't lived up to the expectations of the first-born son of an army general (he had been promoted while I was at Wright State). He didn't really disown me; we just didn't talk. I had worked hard for the past few years, and for the first time in my life, I was self-sufficient and responsible. In a way, I think his visit was a gesture of reward for my efforts as well as an escape from a family Thanksgiving with my mother's sister. Since neither of us was a chef, we went to one of those honey-baked ham stores and purchased a ham, potatoes, and bread and had our own dorm-style Thanksgiving bachelor dinner. It was weird because it was really the first time we had spent quality alone time since my injury almost eight years ago. My mother was thrilled for us, but I was nervous! I was excited yet scared about being with my father. We never talked about how far I had come; the pain I had caused him; or how we felt about my substance abuse, recovery, and admission to grad school. It was near the end of the semester, and for the first time, I was able to report to him that I was succeeding academically in school. What we did talk about was the future, and part of that future was learning to drive again.

Dad had already done preliminary research on the motor vehicle path. He found a couple of Ford dealerships within the greater Pensacola area. Ironically, the chief salesman was a former master sergeant, and of course, he would take care of a general's kid. We bought a blue 1992 Ford E150 van. I was grateful for my father's time and expertise. I had never spent so much money in my life; I nearly hyperventilated. By the end of the weekend our relationship was on solid ground.

I wasn't mentally or physically ready in the past to drive, but I was tired of having every aspect of my life chaperoned or controlled by other people's schedules. Along with my father's help, I identified a number of federal and state programs available to help individuals with disabilities. It's very challenging to know where and how to find the right assistance for a particular need. I was fortunate enough to have spent time in Wright State with other disabled students and learned from their experiences, so I knew that Vocational Rehab (VR) could assist me with a grant and other services in order to adapt the vehicle for my physical needs and help me become gainfully employed. After I mastered the VR program administration, I was able to get Vocational Rehab to assist with the vehicle modifications, a driving therapist, tuition, housing, and books.

The therapist drove from Orlando and spent three days with me assessing my muscles and driving abilities. She wrote a detailed prescription of the appropriate adaptive equipment in order for me to drive. She had her own *MacGyver* tool kit complete with various types of adaptive driving equipment. I was going to get the coolest adaptive equipment – a steering wheel complete with a joy stick to hold my hand and zero resistance (so it was easy to turn the wheel); an automated head rest that included five buttons to control turn signals, wipers, windows, horn, and other essentials; and a gas/brake throttle that took the place of the foot pedals. I was even getting a special driving strap that attached to my chair in lieu of a seatbelt.

The vehicle was shipped to Fort Pierce, Florida, to a guy named Buddy Holiday. He was one of six people in the state of Florida qualified to make such complicated adaptations. Almost six months later, I flew to West Palm Beach with my personal care assistant to finish the modifications and return with my van. Each piece of equipment had to be fine-tuned to my personal needs. For example, my left arm is stronger and has more mobility than my right arm, so the joy stick was placed on the left side of the wheel and van for steering. It was a tiring pro-cess, testing and re-testing and adjusting and testing again for each piece of equipment.

We stayed with George, my friend from high school who was one of the tailbacks from the football team. It was the first time he had seen me since graduation nearly nine years ago. I had to bounce up his steps in order to stay in his condominium and be manually carried in and out of the bathroom because nothing in his house was accessible. He was full of questions, but mostly amazed at how far I had come.

He drove my aide and me to Fort Pierce. We spent the next three days making sure all the equipment was exact once again: testing the weight of the steering wheel; positioning the gas and brake pedal; and learning the locking mechanism for the wheel chair, the lift controls, and everything else. It was re-ally quite amazing – I had purchased a blue van with grey interior. Six months later it had carpet, seats, radio, modified equipment, and a high top roof...it was my *"Enterprise."* The therapist who had organized all of the equipment reappeared at the garage for the final day of fitting. We did a bit of test driv-ing but focused on little things at first: getting in and out of the vehicle, driving around the block, etc. Then it was off to A1-A, nowhere, America; and flat lands. Whoo hoo!!! Second gear, third gear, and even cruise control! I was driving. When we were satisfied that the van was equipped correctly, we had to get it back to Pensacola. Since I didn't have a driver's license, my aide drove, and I was the passenger after all of this prepara-tion. The driver's seat is removable, and the pedals can be used universally. My therapist had scheduled advanced training for me in Pensacola in three weeks so I could acquire my driver's license. She knew me too well: in order to prevent me from driving, she took my driving tri-pin (the way I hold my steering wheel). She did this to ensure that I did not play with my new toy at all until my final training with her in three weeks! We were an hour north of Fort Pierce, and the air conditioner blew out. Having just spent as much money as I had in my entire life, about $52,000, I told my aide to turn around. The vehicle wasn't perfect, and I could hear my father saying, "Take it back." So instead of driving my new van home, we called George for a return trip to the airport. With all the adaptive wires going in and out of the van, someone had messed up the wires to the air conditioning system.

Some two weeks later, the *"Enterprise"* was finally delivered to Pensacola on a flatbed: big, blue, shiny, and mine. Because of the delay, it was another three weeks before the driving instructor could return. All of these delays were killing me. She was scheduled to do 40 hours of Driver's Ed. When she finally arrived, I was quickly able to master the nuances of the vehicle and its size. In less than ten short hours, we drove straight to the DMV to get my license.

The driving evaluator was more than perplexed. I could see that she was surprised and shocked as she watched me finesse my way around the head turn signals, the gears, and the braking mechanisms and masterfully manipulate my equipment. It was encouraging to me when she actually looked at ease. Then there was the three-point parallel parking test. I hit the huge, orange cone on my second turn. We both looked at each other. I was in despair, crushed. She gasped and sorrowfully said, "As much as I would like to pass you, I just can't."

It was a blatant error. I was devastated, and then the bell went off. "Hey! What am I doing parking in a regular parking space anyway?" She looked at me, confused. "I have special handicapped parking spaces that are bigger! You know the ones painted in blue with signs on them!" She leaped out of the van to talk to her supervisor. It was the longest ten minutes of my life. She returned with my driver's license in hand. She also noted that she was going to be modifying the driving assessment for future drivers who would test appropriately for persons with special needs. I now had true independence. No longer would I rely on my friends to take me to the store or to the dentist; I could go on a date unsupervised. I could go to the bank and the video store. I was giddy as could be about this new freedom, but I had significant psychological fears that I had to overcome. For ten years, I had not gone anywhere without another individual by my side. Someone was always with me. Now that I could actually go where I wanted, when I wanted, many new barriers popped up.

I was now learning for the first time how truly inaccessible America was. I found myself spending a lot of time circling a parking lot to find the handicapped parking spot, looking for a curb cut, and wondering how I would enter the building doors. Once inside, how would I handle the goods and payment? I silently thanked my father for faciliting my new found independence. It wasn't just the driving experience my father gave me; it was the courage to participate actively in life.

8

My zeal for more freedom and independence within the world encouraged me to learn more about the ADA. Under this landmark act all public universities had a heightened expectation for accessibility and accommodation of students with disabilities. No longer would moving the classroom to an accessible location be satisfactory. The University of West Florida, a part of the historical south, was not like my barrier free university at Wright State. The two other mobility impaired students and I joined as a team to help the university solve these new legal expectations. We formed the first ever Students with Alternative Needs group. This group was recognized and incorporated into the culture of the university. The school had barriers to remove and we were there to help. As a result of this early leadership, West Florida now has an accessible swimming pool, adaptive sailing program, on campus accessible dormitories, accessible golf cart, and many more common sense independence tools. I have learned that the group is still active 20 years later in excess of 500 members.

As my leadership skills grew and my confidence with academics soared, I took on a new challenge. In the summer of 1992, I began teaching in the *Feet First First Time* program. It was a federal program tailored to bring prevention of spinal cord injuries to high school students. At the time, the leading causes for spinal cord injuries were violence, swimming (diving and surfing), and car accidents. Now that I had my own wheels, I spent once or twice a week teaching neurology, science, and adaptive living to the kids at different schools. I was able to communicate and to share my world with others on an interpersonal level. I was able to help others understand the daily challenges of quadriplegia and perhaps prevent a few souls from joining the club. I became the poster child for my disability. The lead program instructor, seeing my success with the students, asked me to mentor newly-injured quads in the hospital. I was good at it! I was their friend; I was them 10 years ago. I had counted those same holes in the ceiling; I had to learn to rely on someone to take care of me. I was you, and look at me now! I realized that I was really good at bridging gaps between the able-bodied and the disabled. My passion was growing, and so was the cash in my pocket.

Classes were going fairly well, but I was working harder than ever as the competition was harder, and the curriculum required it. Each year in continuing education VR gave me less scholarship money and the extra cash in my pocket wasn't enough. I had to find a full-time job that would coincide with my master's degree in education. The logical employment would be in the school district. I needed to get my teaching certificate. Each county certified their teachers. In my particular case, the old administrative county staff did not know if a quadriplegic could or should be in front of a classroom. I had to get special consideration. I had to be interviewed by the school board. I faced my first barrier in the employment world.

"How will you maintain order in the classroom? How will you execute your lesson plans?" a school board member asked at the meeting, as he looked down at me. The experience was intimidating and hostile, but I kept it together.

"Just like everybody else," was my answer. "There's no reason a teacher has to use the chalk to write on the chalk board; students are very capable of that. New technology that I can utilize has entered the classroom."

I got the job.

While teaching was fun, exciting, accessible, and something I could do well as a quad, I quickly realized that it wasn't going to pay the bills. My salary alone barely met the pay for my personal care, let alone anything else. I shared my dilemma with my faculty members and mentor. They told me to go to Florida State University (FSU) in Tallahassee and get a doctorate. That Christmas, my present to my father was my conditional admissions letter from Florida State University. I was going to get my doctorate; I was going to be the first Harding doctor. We went to a Christmas party, and his best friend General McCaffrey, the most decorated Army soldier at the time, said, "Well, Jim, I never ever thought that JR would become the doctor in the family bloodline." My father grinned with pride and said, "Either did I!"

9

I used the winter of '94 to begin my transition from Pensacola to Tallahassee and Florida State University. Here I was, off starting yet another adventure. They are called adventures because one is never quite certain what is going to happen.

Where would I live? The most logical place, of course, was once again, the university environment. Since the passing of the ADA in 1990, public universities were required to accommodate persons with disabilities. At 26 years of age, I found myself living in a graduate student apartment at the bottom of a freshman dorm. The upside was that I was across the street from the College of Education and a public high school in which I would teach occasionally. I also had an abundance of cheap college labor to assist with my adaptive living. The studio apartment on campus was practical, affordable, and equipped with a roll-in shower to boot. My father drove the U-Haul, this time complete with my bed, stereo, weight machine, TV, and other household goods. As a quad, I had actually acquired a bunch of crap over the years, far different from my first U-Haul trip to Culver.

My adventure took a u-turn when my personal care attendant who had worked for me for two straight years in Pensacola never showed up. He shook my father's hand while closing the doors of the U-Haul and said, "I'll see you in Tally." He just never came. Mom and Dad, the movers, were now also my personal care assistants for four days. It was a big obstacle to handle personal care on the fly and not freak out, and now finding a personal care assistant took precedence over all of our other goals. I had to have faith that it would work out. My parents could only afford the four days in their schedule, and the clock was ticking.

We went to my PCA's cousin's house who happened to live on the other side of Tallahassee, hoping that's where he might be. The cousin opened the door, and we were greeted by screaming kids in the background. He had heard of me, but his cousin was nowhere to be found. He had fallen off the face of the earth. I still don't know where he went or where he is today. As fate would have it, his cousin was actually interested in a part-time job, and I found my personal care attendant. Another complete stranger entered my life as a necessity for survival. It's a leap of faith to take a stranger into your life and trust him.

As things turned out, I could not trust him. About three months into employment, this individual stole from me. The ruse began with a story about losing his paycheck and needing money immediately to pay some bills. Of course I was willing to give him an advance; after all I trusted him with my life. I had to give him my password to the ATM; as a quadriplegic I cannot operate the machine. Two weeks later when I was reviewing my bank statement, $400 was missing. The bank ATM camera caught the whole thing on tape. The bank would not return my money because I willingly gave the number up. I was in a real bind. I had to fire the "chicken thief," but I could not fire him until I could replace him. These kinds of truly bizarre situations are commonplace within the community of disabled people who rely on others. In the end, I did not press charges against him in exchange for his leaving me alone. I was bright enough to dismiss him on payday to recover most of my money. I forced myself to focus on my immediate physical needs and my academics, not the *what if's* of trusting the next PCA. Some things are just beyond one's control.

One thing I could control was my academics. I had been accepted under academic probation because I had a low undergraduate GPA and an average GRE score; I knew I needed to get a 4.0 grade point average to continue and was not eligible for their traditional internships until I had proven myself. Was it fate or one of the gods? After a semester of maintaining a 4.0

GPA, I got two phenomenal pieces of mail in one day: one was from FSU accepting me formally into the doctoral program, and the other was from Ohio expunging my police record. I was released from probation upon leaving Ohio, but I kept in touch with my parole officer and told her about my various successes. A friend applied on my behalf to the state, asking them to remove the stigma attached to my shenanigans from my record, and it paid off. Now that I had my letters, I could begin building my future without having to explain actions and consequences of substance abuse.

FSU received a grant from the federal government to help people with disabilities transition from being college students into being employed professionals. Essentially, I could go to work for anyone who wanted to hire me, and the FSU grant money would pay for it. The max was $10 an hour, 20 hours a week for one year. All I had to do was find someone who was willing to give me a job, a computer, and something to do. VR's scholarship money had been reduced even lower, and this program was a huge help with my finances. I was able to find a position in Governor Chiles' office with an emphasis on higher education. It matched my graduate work in the field of higher education, so I found the ideal job. I became an intern handling the public's money for private universities and colleges for the governor's administration. Now I had my own graduate internship. I had to keep a journal on my job hunt: how many people I met with, how many hours it took, and finally where I eventually landed and what my job entailed. The first day of the job, my supervisor told me to read the public laws overseeing the public university system for the state of Florida. On the very first page, I read about the board of regents and the ONE student regent spot. "Regent: one who rules." I knew immediately I wanted this post.

I went to my supervisor an hour later with a big grin on my face and asked, "What about this regent position?"

She smiled back, noting my youthful enthusiasm, and said, "One out of 300,000 students make it. Qualification isn't difficult, but receiving the governor's appointment is quite another matter."

I quietly went about doing my job following the legislative budget process, the governor's recommendations, and the legislative education committee hearings. Legislative staffs are like children; they are to be seen but not heard except when spoken to. It's astounding the response you get when you call the University of Miami and tell them you are with "the Governor's office." It's amazing how quickly they put you through or return your call. I learned firsthand how powerful elected officials are and how they impact our daily lives. I still recall watching one of the education sub-committees debate whether or not Algebra 1 should be a high school graduation requirement for the state of Florida. I was beyond shell shocked; I didn't know choices like that were made. I struggled through all that algebra because of their decisions.

Out of the blue, my friend from Pensacola and State Representative, Buzz Ritchie, came to see how I was doing. He was now the Chairman of the Appropriations Committee. This was a big deal. Everyone in the office was buzzing with curiosity.

After jovial chit chat and life updates, he asked me if there was anything he could do for me.

"Well, yes, sir." I said, "I want to work for you next semester."

He looked at his assistant blankly, not knowing how to answer such a direct comment. She then said, "You are the chairman; you can do anything you want."

"Well, then, JR, write me up a proposal, and we'll talk about it."

I grinned.

Within two weeks, I was working for the House of Appropriations chairman and the House of Representatives. I was assisting the chair in private education for the State of Florida. Of the $60 billion state budget, approximately $1 billion went to various private institutions of higher learning. My job was to analyze the budget for these institutions and make recommendations to the Appropriations Committee.

Halfway through the legislative process my persistence paid off, I earned the honor of interviewing with Governor Chiles for the position of student regent. There are 15 regent members, and only one of them is a student, representing all universities across the state. Politically, this was a major coup because Florida State had just had a student regent, and the other local university's student (from FAMU) was in the process of finishing his term. Therefore, geographically, my part of the state was not in consideration. Tallahassee had its fair share of representation, and the position is generally allocated to the governor's children or grandchildren or close friends. Lightning struck and we realized with the help of the university presidents from West Florida and Florida State, that I could become the first ever candidate from West Florida and the first ever to represent Florida's disabled population. At the time, there were about 1.5 million students enrolled in colleges and universities in Florida, and approximately 10 percent of those students had disabilities. In 12 short years, public higher education had grown a long way with the matriculation of students with disabilities. Now there was actually a need for a disabled voice to speak. The interview with the governor was the first of its kind for me. It was surreal. I was actually meeting the governor, and I wanted him to do something for me. I had to convince him to break political tradition and take a chance on me and give the disabled population something it needed: a voice. The chief of staff led me into the office; it was late spring/early summer, and the legislative session had completed. The governor was in a white polo shirt and khaki pants. I was in my brand new suit; this was maybe the second time I had ever worn one. The part that settled me and made me feel at ease was the governor's dog. The little fur ball was jumping in the air and playing toss with its master. The dog was just a hair bigger than the contemporary purse poodle. Between tosses with the dog, the Governor asked, "So you want to be my Student Regent?"

I said with a crackling voice, "Yes, sir!"

He proceeded to ask why.

I then went into my well-rehearsed dissertation of what I knew about the system, what it lacked, and how I would lead by example.

Twenty minutes later, he shook my hand.

"Thank you for coming, JR. You are an impressive young man!"

I left the room with uncertainty, kicking myself, wishing I had said this or that and immediately sat down and wrote my obligatory thank you note. I must have written it three or four times so he could actually read my disabled hand writing.

Soon thereafter, my special internship concluded, and I was once again just a student pursuing a doctorate in education. Three months had passed since I had interviewed with the governor. I followed up with the chancellor, Dr. Charles Reed, on several occasions inquiring if there was any news.

"Patience, young man, these things take time," the chancellor would tell me.

As soon as I was getting really discouraged, the phone rang.

"JR, this is President Sandy D'Alemberte of FSU."

My heart stopped, and with my voice crackling again, I said, "Yes?"

He began talking freely to me about the university's needs and asked me about my experiences as a student.

"What would you like to see changed?"

Classrooms still weren't accessible; on-campus housing needed improvement; and even getting to his old office was a challenge.

Most of the time professionals would humor me and talk to me because it was the "right" thing to do. Now all of a sudden, the Governor's VIP's were truly interested in my opinions because they thought I had something to contribute.

The phone had been ringing off the hook so I didn't pay much attention to the late afternoon call. I broke away from a book and the warm sun and barely made it in time to catch the last ring.

"Could you hold for the Governor please?" Oh my, this is it. My heart pounded.

The Governor got on the line, said some nice things and then asked if I was ready to serve the State of Florida.

I almost jumped out of my chair with enthusiasm. I couldn't believe it! I'm a student regent! I got it! And I grinned.

His last words to me were, "Just tell them what you think."

By September 1996, I was the newly-appointed student regent for a four billion-dollar, ten-university organization with 300,000 students. And the circus began: newspapers, TV reporters … everybody wanted to know who this 27-year-old graduate student was. On paper and the press releases, I came across as an able body. Once they found out I was disabled, their interests peaked, and the questions came flying. Could I represent the entire student body or just those with disabilities? Had anyone with a disability ever been a regent? How could someone so young effectively govern? I was the youngest by almost 30 years. While I was elated and very satisfied, the job was still very abstract to me. I did not know what I had volunteered for. I had worked hard for this appointment but, in fact, really did not embrace the importance of my achievement.

In preparation for my first meeting at the University of North Florida (UNF) in Jacksonville, I went a day early to meet the president, the student body president, and the faculty to receive briefings on the board agenda as it related to UNF. As I pulled into the administrative parking lot, I was greeted by the president and personally escorted into the conference room. They were eager to know more about me and how they might shape my views on policy. The following day we had our first meeting. I soon began to realize the pomp and circumstance that went along with being a regent. "One who made the rules." I loved it! I was seated at the head of the table surrounded by all the vice presidents and the deans. I looked around the horseshoe-shaped table, and it was more like the Knights of the Round Table. There I was among all the university presidents and a part of the king's court. Roll was taken, a quorum was called to order, and my reign began. I was thrown before a fast-moving train and was expected to jump on. Toward the end of the second day, having listened to a debate in my class of higher learning for the past two years, I realized I had an advantage. I grew the courage to raise my hand, and the whole room was silent.

"The Student Regent wants to be recognized."

Shit. I was about to chime in on a major policy argument; I was scared to death. I politely summarized two or three other regent perspectives and then anchored my comments on what I knew to be true from my class discussions on the current topic. At the conclusion of my argument, one of the other regents made a motion to accept my argument and policy direction. I had just made my first contribution to the State of Florida and my first policy decision. I was king – *King* Regent.

At the end of the meeting, the supportive regent, the one who made the motion, came up to me, put his arm around me as a fellow southern boy, and said, "Welcome to the board. I love the way you put the other regents in their place! You will not be like the past student regents. You will make a difference." I grinned.

I wasn't really certain what cliff I had fallen off of, but I certainly liked the landing. The board had given me a formal office next to the president. I declined and requested one closer to my classes, and before I knew it, I had an office right next to my professors. My mail was addressed to the Honorable Regent. The cherry on top arrived three days before the home football game. The president and his leadership cordially invited me and a guest to his sky box. I learned that I would no longer need my cheap student tickets. The sky box offer would be available as long as I was regent.

Another perk of being Regent was getting National Championship tickets. FSU football was on a amazing run during the 90s. We had 14 top 5 finishes. Anyone who follows college football knows how hard it is to get championship tickets. If you are not a major Booster, you have to buy them on the secondary market, generally for way too much money.

As Regent, I got a phone call from the Vice President's office, "Have you had a chance to decide upon your tickets and housing for the championship game? How many tickets would you require, and how many hotel rooms do you need?"

It was a good feeling not to stand in line or haggle over price.

I said to the secretary, "Really? Do I need to answer today?"

"No sir, take as much time as you need. You are limited however, to four tickets and two rooms."

I immediately called one of my best friends Mike, and he said, "Get the hell out of here! When are we going to New Orleans?"

FSU and the University of Florida were playing in the 1997 Nokia Sugar Bowl Championship game. We got to stay in the team's hotel, VIP parking, attend parties, all of it presented on an itinerary left in my room. It was good to be Regent. Sadly, Danny Wuerffel and the Florida Gators upstaged my Seminoles.

I was excelling beyond my wildest dreams. My academics were excellent. I was raising the bar as to what it meant to be a Student Regent. I had co-authored the student affairs section of the new five year master plan for the State University System. I was driving; I could go anywhere. I learned to scuba dive and water ski. I started public speaking. The ADA laws were taking root in all aspects of my life and I was having fun. I was so independent that even I forgot that I was a quadriplegic.

10

My brother finally announced his engagement to his Swedish girlfriend. The shock wasn't that he was getting married but that they wanted to get married in Sweden! Such a vacation would challenge my abilities. *Why not?*, I thought to myself. I can do anything. The timing was perfect, I decided to take two weeks off the pensive labors of my dissertation and regent duties and planned my international trip. I decided to save a few bucks and fly out of Orlando instead of Tallahassee. I drove to Orlando and picked up my personal care assistant. Pat was a former aide who lived in Orlando and was able to take some time off to make my trip possible. Who wouldn't want a paid trip to Sweden?

The wedding was on a remote island in an old renaissance castle. Even my family's expectations of my abilities were not those of a quadriplegic, as they had me traveling on ferries, crossing castle moats, driving in modified delivery vans, and being carried up flights of castle stairs. It was a pleasant 10 days with the family exploring the countryside and going to places no other quadriplegic had dreamed of. Summertime in Sweden is breathtaking. The colors were vibrant and bright just like the post cards suggest. As I watched my brother say his vows, I thought to myself, *someday this could be me.*

It was a long flight home, and I had been going non-stop. Thank God I was able to charm the stewardess into bumping me up to first class with my piercing blue eyes. I was so excited to get home and get back to work. My prospectus had been approved by the committee for the dissertation stage, and now all I had to do was put it all together. Who would have thought I would be a Doctor of Education? That's something no one EVER expected I would do.

Once back in the states, I rested briefly at Pat's house and was up at the crack of dawn the next morning. He thanked me for a superb vacation and wished me well. I took off alone onto the Florida Turnpike. I was looking forward to my lunch appointment with Jimmy, a bud from college. I was excited to share doctorate horror stories with him and hear about his program; he was attending the University of Florida with an emphasis on molecular biology. I was making good time on the empty highway, looking for the merge onto I-75.

The fuzz on the radio station grew annoying. I desperately hit the radio button again in search of relief from country music twang. Nothing. Again...search.

On my fourth attempt at reaching for the search button, I suddenly felt the drunk bumps rattle the van underneath, shaking me violently. My exhausted body went into rigorous muscle spasms. I saw the empty highway turn and heard the noise, the screeching. The van tumbled four times. I went over the steering wheel and through the windshield. The crunching of the steel scraping across the concrete came to a standstill. I thought to myself that it would be over in a minute, and then I blacked out. I awoke next to the smoking and crushed van, face down in the median of the highway. Possibly the gods thought my years as a quadriplegic to be insufficient as they had more obstacles and challenges in store for me. I spit dirt out from my mouth and waited for help.

Jimmy was distraught, wondering where I was. I was never this late and always true to schedule, always a planner. He called Pat and asked him if I had left on time.

"He left here bright and early; something must be wrong."

"You call the highway patrol, and I'll try the hospitals. Call me back when you know something." Jimmy called the hospitals. Nothing.

"An accident...blue ford van...is he ok?" Pat asked.

"What do you mean you can't reveal his condition...screw it...where did they take him?"

"Wildwood Regional Medical Clinic? Why isn't he in Gainesville? Oh, forget it."

He hung up the phone, and his fingers trembled and shook while dialing Jimmy.

"I'm on my way – meet you there!"

"Young man, you are at the Wildwood Clinic because you have been in a car accident."

I glared at him, lifted my left eyebrow slightly, and demanded, "Take me to Gainesville; call Dr. Thacker and tell him I'm on my way."

The doctor pathetically proclaimed with his coffee breath, "Possibly you don't understand the seriousness of your injuries, young man. You have two broken legs, one broken shoulder, and a spinal cord injury."

I interrupted, "Get me a phone." I knew this clinic didn't have a clue about how to handle my needs.

Meanwhile, Pat and Jimmy hooked up in the lobby. Sneaking past the nurses, all Pat and Jimmy could see were two big feet hanging over the end of a gurney adorned with a starched white sheet on top.

"Nah," they thought to themselves, "He couldn't be dead." They were actually relieved once they heard my voice and demands. Whatever was wrong, my mouth still worked.

They heard me bark again at the doctor.

"So, already giving orders, huh?" Pat asked. "You're going to be just fine," he smiled.

Walking into my line of sight, they asked what they could do.

"First, call my parents, and second, call the University of Florida because the doctor is an idiot," I said.

As a State University Student Regent, I had a personal relationship with the president of the University of Florida. I knew I could count on him. I had thoroughly embraced the pomp and circumstance of being a regent: the reserved parking spot, the fancy cocktail parties, and, of course, the President's Box at the football games. I would take friends and occasionally dates there to impress them. The president had told me repeatedly that if there was anything I ever needed to be sure to reach out to him. I don't think he ever imagined I would call him for a space at his hospital.

Pat hated to leave this kind of a message for my parents as General Harding and his wife Vicki were not home from Sweden yet. His next call was to the University and the President. Almost immediately thereafter, we could hear the phone ringing at the nurse's station. It was the President of the University instructing the nurse to send me to their campus hospital in Gainesville even though they were at full capacity and engulfed in bad weather. The President had made special arrangements for a transfer and somehow made space for me. When I learned of my success and the president's coming to my aide, I grinned like the Cheshire Cat. It felt good to have some control despite being broken in pieces. Before I knew it, I was loaded for yet another ride in an ambulance and succumbed to the power of the morphine.

11

Vicki and Jim were exhausted. Planning a wedding in a different country was more than Vicki had anticipated. Overall, she was pleased with the outcome. There was still a DC reception to host on behalf of the newlyweds. Jim dropped the suitcases on the floor and immediately took the dog out. Vicki perused the house and surveyed its orderliness. She found a few water stains on the counter that the cleaning lady had missed, wiped the counter down, and noticed the flashing orange light on the phone. "You have four new messages." The first was the florist reminding her that the final deposit was due tomorrow when they would meet one final time at the Army Navy Country Club to finalize the décor. The second was Pat. Vicki listened to the message three times before she completely understood the call. She never listened to the remaining messages. She had a flight booked to Gainesville before Jim returned with the dog.

She arrived the next day at the Gainesville hospital and was pleased to know that her son had insisted on being treated there. Her first meeting was to be with the doctor so that she could prepare herself before seeing her first born son. She had become accustomed to the phone calls and emergency rooms with her son throughout the years. She was a strong woman who loved her son dearly but never coddled him or spoiled him. She wished that he didn't always have to jump into everything, taking life by the horns and, therefore, learning most everything the hard way. They felt it best that he go to boarding school at the age of seven for the necessary discipline and education he required. She recalled the phone conversation from the headmaster of the Oakland Farm School in Virginia, "Mrs. Harding, this is Joseph Clark, the Headmaster of the Oakland Farm School. Your son was taken to the hospital. He was hit in the mouth with a baseball bat. He was knocked unconscious, has 14 stitches in the mouth, but is going to live. He seems pleased with the doctor's orders of drinking milkshakes."

Over the years, her son had enough stitches to connect a quilt from California to New York City. The unspoken rule was to only call her after he got cleaned up. She was somewhat tickled remembering the incidents as she prepared herself for her son's latest incident.

"Your son has two broken legs, one broken shoulder, and a severed spinal cord injury at the C-6 level. While his bones will heal; his degree of paralysis is unknown." This was all the doctor could share with her because her oldest son was no longer a dependent, and the federal health care rules had changed. He was an adult, and only he could direct his care now.

This was the cruelest form of *Groundhog's Day*. I was unable to talk because they had crammed a respirator down my throat. My mother would point to letters in the alphabet, and I would blink my eyes on the correct letter in order to communicate with her. It was a very tedious task for such a talker as I. I was frustrated beyond belief with this slow and painful process; there was no room for details. Sentences were short and quick. The effects of the morphine made it even harder for me to stay focused. Once again, the only view of the room was the ceiling or the floor when they would rotate my body like a hot dog on a rotisserie. They would poke me, stick me, and even prod me, but my only feeling was awareness. Again, the time of day was marked by the shift changes of nurses and technicians. I recall being in this situation once before fifteen years earlier in Chicago.

This time it was not the priest reading the last rights to me, but my very real struggle with ICU psychosis bringing me closer to death. I was awake for blurred moments at three hour intervals before the hallucinations took over. The drugs would take a hold of my mind as quickly as they dulled the pain. I had re-occurring nightmares. The medical staff, with their sterile gloves and surgical masks, played leading roles in my mind's tragic scientific horror film. They were conducting experimental medical procedures on me with my family's consent. I thought they were harvesting my bones and parts for others who had a better chance of survival. I imagined I heard my mother say, "He would never want to live like this! A quad is dependent on a respirator and others, bound to a wheel chair. He can't handle this. We need to pull his life support so we can use what parts are still intact."

Sweat balls rolling down over my ears caused my neck hairs to stand on end. I feared for my life and couldn't believe my family was going to take my heart and my eye balls. They were going to steal everything that still might be in working order.

"Now what?" I thought to myself. *"Oh no!"* They are *moving me...help!"* I cringed as I looked at the dark grey cement walls.

A single light above me warmed my face. *"This must be where they pull my parts out."* I refused to close my eyes fearful they would never voluntarily open again. I did not want to sleep as I thought I would never wake again. My mother would watch my body spasm during these hallucinations for hours. She would try to comfort me with a cold compress applied to my forehead, but nothing brought me back to reality. She was angered because the physicians wouldn't give her more details. She felt helpless against the new medical rules of HIPPA.

Hours later, I did indeed awake in another room, and the smell of metal sterilization was still there. It was a different ICU corridor. There were no cement walls, only a different white ceiling with thousands of tiny white holes and the tile floor with wax build up and occasional scuffs. As I lay there, I wondered which body parts were missing as all of my tubing had been moved. I still could not feel below the neck and didn't know which parts might have been harvested away. I glared at the nurses and doctors, knowing that they were indeed part of the continuing plan to harvest my parts. My anxiety was running rapid. Still unable to speak, my psychosis took me into unimaginable depths of confusion and horror.

I thought I had heard my brother's voice. He was addressing the doctor.

"He has been unplugged for hours. Why won't he die?" My brother reached for the pillow and placed it on my head.

In actuality, the nurse was gently placing the pillow behind my head and explaining to my mom that they were taking out the respirator. I was being choked. I felt the harshness in my throat, gagging mucus. "No!" I cried. "No!" Vicki jumped when she heard my screams of, "I don't want to die." She had no idea what I was talking about. Dying? What was wrong with him? She was in a frenzy when she spoke to the hospital staff. She wanted answers!

"I'm sorry Ma'am, your son is covered under the HIPPA agreement, and I am unable to tell you anything about the condition of your son, in particular the medicines and treatment being provided for him." The nurse stated verbatim and without compassion. "We have implemented these standards in order to protect and guard against misuse of individually identifiable health information. May I suggest you speak with your son?"

"Speak to him?" She screamed. "My God! I haven't been able to speak to him since I arrived, you..." She was furious! She was distractedly grateful and relieved when she saw Jimmy coming down the hall by the nurse's station. She had an unbarring weight of guilt encompassing her. She intended to leave; she still had her other son's wedding party to attend to in DC.

He was holding a stuffed Seminole doll with an attached "get well soon" balloon. They walked into his hospital room together.

"MOM!" I shouted. "You can't leave...they want my eyes...don't let them take my blue eyes."

My mother explained to Jimmy that the past couple of days had been horrific. "He doesn't know what's fiction or nonfiction. I have no idea what's wrong with him. He's not himself."

"Well let's see what's up," Jimmy said. The sound of Jimmy's voice immediately brought me relief. Because Jimmy had not been present for the hallucination escapade and had not played a role in the horror show, his presence comforted me. He was like a lighthouse guiding one through a storm. I immediately looked into his eyes and said, "Thank God you are here. They are trying to kill me..."

Jimmy could sense and see the fear in my face. I jumbled my thoughts and sentences, trying to explain to him the doctor's plans and my family's true intentions. He showed no shock and absorbed all my nonsense. He fed me ice chips to combat the dehydration. He watched me fade in and out of consciousness, my eyes wandering rapidly under my eyelids. He excused himself and reassured his prompt return. Jimmy was getting a PhD in molecular biology, and because of his training and studies, he determined that I was having a very bad experience with the morphine. He found an attending physician and described the situation. Remarkably, he was able to convince the doctor to change the pain medication. They compromised on something that could comfort me but not feed into my fears and the psychosis. Jimmy was a tremendous friend that day. He stayed for 36 hours and untangled the fictitious reality of my morphine nightmare, and my mother headed home to the wedding reception without guilt. She dreaded having to put on a happy exterior to face the world when she knew that her son was in turmoil. But the party must go on, and she decided it was best not to tell family and friends of the accident in fear of ruining the event.

Things seemed to be better, and Jimmy had to get back to his studies. Jimmy felt a sense of relief when he started his car, knowing that the new medication would facilitate a safer sleep and that I was stable again.

I awoke in a panic. There was gurgling, and I was gasping for air. I mentally reached for the button knowing quite well that I was paralyzed and would never succeed. "I've got to, oh

God, somebody help me... I can't reach it. I can't move....Oh God, help me," I cried to myself.

Thankfully, my roommate sensed my restlessness and called for the nurse. My lungs were filling with fluid. My heart was pounding, and my eyes were shockingly white. The nurse hurried into the room and quickly started poking and prodding before paging the respiratory therapist. I heard the rattling of wheels and saw the plastic tubes hanging from a wire. The therapist pounded on my back and lungs in hopes of loosening the phlegm. Then he lubricated a catheter and inserted it down my nose and into my lungs. Four inches of milky slime were sucked out of my chest. Every four hours, he returned, turning me in different directions so that the phlegm was easier to cough up. Three days passed filled with pumping, sucking, coughing, and liquid expulsion. My only concern was breathing. I didn't want to sleep for fear of my lungs filling up. I exhausted myself. There was no energy or strength to think beyond the next three hours. The therapist had to switch between my left and right nostrils as each was raw and chapped. When I was tilted downward, my head to the floor and my feet above me, all I could see was the white scum dripping into a clear plastic container. Each day consisted of a rotation to prevent pressure sores and adjusting my view of the scum jug.

After a week, my blood gases finally stabilized, and the gurgling subsided. Because of the changes in health care, I was fast tracked to rehab. I was off on another ambulance ride across town. This time I had a stuffed Seminole, two broken legs, a broken shoulder, a second spinal cord injury, and a new box of "get well" cards.

I was thrilled to see my mother again. She returned from my brother's reception almost immediately. My brother and her closest friends had no idea of the weight she carried with her that night as she chose not to mention my second injury to anyone. There was nothing any of them could do, and she did not want to spoil the event. She brought some of my things from Virginia and tried to warm the new rehab room. Although

71

she had brought some of my stuff, there was no changing the fact that I was in rehab and not in my self-sufficient bachelor pad at FSU. Now that I had recovered from my psychosis and a collapsed lung, I knew I wasn't dying anymore. I was really, really mad when I was able to grasp my situation fully. Both my legs were in full casts; my left arm was secured to my chest; and the frickin' halo was screwed back onto my head. I had minimal mobility in my one good arm and was unable to use the remote control for the TV or answer the phone. I was a complete mess.

There was never a choice of giving up. I had now cheated death for a second time, and living was now my goal; I was at the starting blocks again. The gun goes off, and you go. So I went through my rehab with the same zest for life all over again.

I hated being alone because it gave me time to think. It gave me too much time to feel. Yes, quadriplegics do feel. I would call my mother every night, listen to her voice, and cry. It was a long, constant, inner cry for hours. It pained my mother so, to listen, to have no answers, but just hold her son across the invisible wires and help me slowly begin to heal.

During the day when my brain and emotions were otherwise occupied, I somehow became an inspiration to others in my room and throughout the hospital. The staff and families looked up to me. They admired my determination. They all felt that I was filled with endless efforts to recover. I often shared my knowledge of independence, healthcare, and community resources with others. I had learned it all during my first injury. I had a strong outer shell but still suffered my own insecurities. I didn't know if I could handle a higher level of paralysis than what I experienced those first 15 years. I had made peace once with myself and God. Could I do it again? Unbeknownst to the staff and my new paralyzed friends, I was struggling with things like the crane. I hated the crane that moved me. It was a metal claw that clasped my paralyzed body, hurling me around like a piece of cargo. Because I was 6'5", 230 pounds, and had two broken legs, the nurses just weren't able to move me. My showers that I had taken for granted everyday, were now far and few. I was reduced to a bed bath again. I had to wait an extra two weeks for a fitted wheelchair because I was so big and had two long legs in casts sticking out. I had not been in a wheelchair at all since the second injury. I had only been toted around on a stretcher and the crane because nothing would fit me. So when the chair arrived and I saw the high back wheelchair complete with a neck brace, I crumbled. It was a slap in the face; I was more paralyzed now, and sadly, I missed what limited movement I used to have. As motivation, I had my wheelchair from home, the cool sports chair, sent to me at rehab. Each day I would tell everyone that I would return to MY chair one day and leave the La-Z-Boy on wheels in the dust.

I was an adult. I had adult responsibilities that needed to be attended to. One of the biggest challenges I now faced was managing and documenting the incoming doctor bills. My attending physician reminded me that because of the changes in medical care measures in cost and treatments, they could be required to discharge me on any given Friday. The medical care benchmarks were strictly abstract, not on a personal basis. They thought I was recovering; little did they know I still couldn't even brush my teeth.

I was overwhelmed when a story was printed about me in the local newspaper, not because I had my fifteen minutes of fame but because my friend's brother brought the article to his college lecture hall and asked for volunteers. Soon my lonely evening hours were filled with cheerleaders of all shapes and sizes – which I really liked. We practiced writing and washing my face – not my whole face, just my chin to start. I learned how to change the channel on the remote and sneak a peek down my volunteers' shirts. A milestone was re-learning how to use the phone. I finally managed to hit the speaker phone button in time before the caller would hang up. I hired another college recruit to take over my personal life at home. I had to give up absolute control. I was still bitter because my previous aide had stolen from me. The new assistant had access to my savings, my bank account, absolutely everything. I was counting on her to restore my faith in trust...I had no other choice. She paid all my bills, including the stacks of medical bills now totaling more than a half of a million dollars. With the team in place, I was able to refocus on my ultimate goal: my doctorate. I was working remotely through the internet and e-mail at first, but then I challenged the university with a request for an academic accommodation to make the system faster and simpler. The university was enthusiastic about my request and installed a hyperlink between two different university systems so that I could access my research and manipulate my source data without having to cut and paste. I was analyzing graduation rates between traditional university students and community college transfers as it related to time of degree and grade point average. Basically, my research would determine if the institution where a student began attending college made a difference.

Before my accident, I had three personal care assistants. Two of them were college students who required extra beer and girlfriend money, so I was able to let them go. But the third, Eric, had made me his full-time job. Because of his dedication and loyalty, I kept him on the payroll, and he would drive down every weekend and work with me. Back in Tallahassee we had new challenges including two broken legs, a broken shoulder and did not use a lift to transfer. Therefore, he had to be retrained in caring for me in preparation for the minute's notice to return home whenever the HMO decided to kick me out. My legs finally healed enough to bend, and I was able to get into MY wheelchair. My arm sling was removed, and I found that I could actually push **my** chair. I was using my sport chair as promised. I grinned proudly.

Three weeks before the November election, I had a surprise visitor. Candidate Jeb Bush came to watch one of the Florida State football games with me. I had served as leader for the Young Republican vote, and he hadn't forgotten me. We were continually interrupted by fans, potential voters, and gawkers, and he would politely tell them that he was just taking some time to visit a friend. We talked about family, politics, and my progress. I was blown away by his compassion to make time for ME with the election so close. Knowing I had a part to play in the State of Florida gave me great confidence and added strength for the completion of my dissertation. I promised my friends, family, dissertation committee, and fellow regents that I would make it home for the Florida/Florida State game, the biggest rival game of the year.

12

I t was time. Discharge day – two beautiful words. The day was filled with hugs, kisses, and even tears. I certainly had left my mark on the institution. I was their first ever two-time quadriplegic. The nurses were really going to miss me. They adored my smile and my effervescent blue eyes but mostly my determination and spirit. It was odd, packing up my worldly belongings from my home for the past 90 days. Discharge sounds great in theory, but when you actually sign papers, they release you, wash their hands of you, and leave you at the curb. How was I going to get home? My dear friend, Jimmy, rescued me again. He and my aide threw me into the back seat of his Ford Van and tied me down with seat belts and bungee cords. On every bump and turn, I would roll, twist, and turn like the fallen groceries in the trunk of a car. The color was drained from my face. The fear, the memory of my crash encompassed me. It was the first time I had been in any vehicle besides an ambulance since my van rolled on the turnpike. I finally arrived home at my apartment. I confidently grinned to myself as I re-entered my fully-accessible apartment. I was home a week earlier than the doctors and friends had anticipated.

I had to get acclimated to my new routine. My system of care had been changed because of my second spinal cord injury. My daily program now included more physical therapy including morning and afternoon stretching. I had to struggle through the many medical bills and other household chores, all while completing my dissertation. Just as soon as my well-oiled machine started to tick, I was told that my graduate dormitory was scheduled for remodeling and that as much as the university cared for me, I would have to vacate my accessible apartment by June 1999.

That March I had to defend my dissertation in front of the committee including the Dean of Education, three members of the Department of Educational Leadership, and one outside committee member. The defense of a dissertation is an academic dog and pony show. It's a form of academic hazing. All who have written one understand that when you get to the defense position, you have already passed. It is one last time for the candidate to grovel and demonstrate his or her prowess at the subject in hand. I was still nervous as shit, and it's not done until all members of the committee sign and admit you into the club.

The chairman of the committee, Dean Miller, was the first to congratulate me.

The other committee members followed, introducing themselves without title and using their first names. It's really rather surreal because I had spent the past 12 years in college trying to become one, and suddenly everyone was calling me Doctor.

With my academic work successfully behind me, it was time to focus on my new challenge of finding a place to live. Of course, I couldn't live just anywhere. I had to have a roll-in shower, a ramp to enter the property, a spare bedroom for my personal care assistant, and those are only a few of the must-haves. Should I rent and then find a house, thus moving twice? Do I find a house right away? Driving the fundamental dilemma was what I could afford. I needed a job too!

Because of my regent experience, two years running the state university system, and one year serving as the student affairs committee chairman, I received offers to work at Florida Atlantic University and Florida Gulf Coast University. They were excited about recruiting me. I knew I could do the job, but deep down I was scared. I had only been home for five months. I was still receiving physical therapy. I had not yet begun to drive again. It would be many months with other people driving me around until I gained enough physical strength to once again safely drive my modified vehicle with hand controls. Could I really pack it all up, begin working in a strange environment, replicate my disability infrastructure, and find a place to live?

Perhaps Zeus threw a fireball of opportunity my way. March through May is the annual legislative session, and in late April, the legislature decided to privatize Vocational Rehab. With this bill signed, Governor Bush suggested to the commissioner of education that Dr. Harding was the man for the job.

Out of nowhere, I had a job, and I could go to the bank for a loan. Because I had been frugal, I had some money left from my grandmother's inheritance. With that money, the Social Security Pass Program (the government allows persons with disabilities to save money toward a one-time purchase without having the money negatively impact the benefits program), and my new salary, I could borrow up to 200,000 dollars with a 20 percent down payment.

With the help of a realtor who understood my adaptive needs, I went house hunting. Because I was unable to jump into her two-door Mercedes, she was required to drive the modified van that my insurance replaced. We went through every single neighborhood in Tallahassee. Of course, I couldn't be too far out of town because I had my infrastructure to worry about. Over a three-week window, the realtor and I managed to make a six house short list. My father and I would examine this short list during his upcoming visit at my doctoral graduation.

The FSU spring commencement ceremony was scheduled for May 5, 1999. I was looking forward to this graduation ceremony because it was my first formal graduation experience since the summer of 1984 when I graduated from high school. Family and friends from South Florida and as far as Texas all came to see me on my big day! Everyone had played a part in my successes, and they were personally taking pride in my achievements. It was really going to be a spectacular day.

We all marched into the auditorium and took our seats. When US Attorney General Janet Reno, who was the commencement speaker, actually came off the stage to shake my hand in front of 10,000 people, I trembled. I knew then and there that I would always stand out! It would be my moral and ethical obligation to represent the cross-disability community with dignity and professional standards no matter where I went.

Because I was unaccustomed to university graduation ceremonies, I did not appreciate the order of things, the time involved, and the sheer number of spectators. In this case, the local Civic Center was standing room only, holding somewhere between 10,000 and 12,000 people. I was getting bored even though it was my day; 2,500 undergraduate names had been read aloud. Each one of those individuals entered across the stage and shook the university president's hand. Then the readings of the 500 plus master's degree students' names were read, and they too meandered across the stage. Finally, some two hours later, the doctoral students, the grand finale, had come! It was my time! There I sat in the front row on the left hand side, waiting for my name to be called. Finally, my name was called, but before actually articulating "James Raymond Harding II," the president had a nice little story to add regarding courage, determination, leadership, and service. Up the ramp I went, rolling ever so slowly to enjoy every minute (I could see my parents smiling from the VIP's spectator section); I shook the president's hand and turned, faced all 10,000 people, and received my doctoral hood from my lead professor. She barely stood taller than I sat, and it was difficult to actually knight me in the academic manner, but we managed.

It was a shock not only to me but also to those around me. Even strangers such as Janet Reno were amazed at my achievement. I was proud to be the first of the Hardings to be honored with such a title. I rolled ever so slowly, my version of meandering, up to my father. I pushed the degree toward him, smiled, and said, "So, now what?"

Epic

A year after graduation, during a recognition dinner from the University of West Florida, my mentor, professor, and friend delivered the following address (To be sung to the strains of the Beowulf Rap):

A mini Epic for JR

So come we all to fete JR
Whose wheeling and dealing
                    have brought him far--
From Argo days alive with fun,
Where papers and reading
                    came second to sun.
In mood alteration he never had peer,
Spreading candor and humor and limitless beer.
From the dorm room, the Rat, or even Seville,
Ol' JR was known for his raconteur skill.
But his journey took on a mythic dimension
In a myth course with me that consumed his attention.
Crossing his Threshold to a long Road of Trials
JR took to his studies, put aside Wasteland styles.
Well, at least, this young hero Resurrected his goal
To make differences daily without being droll.
His heroship flourished, his followers legion;
Champion'd Disability causes, a pioneer in this region
Then to the Seminoles, to forge shared allegiance;
A Panhandle hero, Seated on the board of Regents.
Though his Trials continued, JR bested them all--
Atonement and honor make him seated SO TALL.

Ron & Mary

Epilogue

It's been more than a decade since the last emergency phone call. I taught JR how to feed himself not once, but on three different occasions. It was like giving birth to the same child over and over again. Each time a different place, a new city, and new challenges, but throughout, the constant was my love for him. Although he is confined to a wheelchair, I have never met anyone with his will and ability to push forward. After getting his doctorate, he continued on his journey of breaking down barriers for the disabled. He has received two presidential appointments, seven gubernatorial appointments, and has served on several different boards. He is my inspiration when I am down and feeling blue. I think of how he faces each day with enthusiasm and drive. When he smiles, he grins like no other. Because of his leadership, others have followed.

My best friend asked me the other day if I was fulfilled. Was my life complete? And I turned to her and said, "The only thing left is that I hope JR will find someone willing to share his life with him. Someone to love."

The rumbling above started once more, and the lightning bolt shot out again – but this time into the heart. The phone did ring, but this time it wasn't an emergency. "Mom, I'm getting married!" he said... And I cried!

26600164R00050

Made in the USA
Lexington, KY
12 October 2013